Four Corners

Jack C. Richards · David Bohlke

3A

Student's Book

CAMBRIDGE
UNIVERSITY PRESS

CAMBRIDGE UNIVERSITY PRESS
Cambridge, New York, Melbourne, Madrid, Cape Town, Singapore,
São Paulo, Delhi, Dubai, Tokyo, Mexico City

Cambridge University Press
32 Avenue of the Americas, New York, NY 10013-2473, USA

www.cambridge.org
Information on this title: www.cambridge.org/9780521127271

First published 2012

Printed in Hong Kong, China, by Golden Cup Printing Company Limited

A catalog record for this publication is available from the British Library.

ISBN 978-0-521-12727-1 Full Contact 3A with Self-study CD-ROM
ISBN 978-0-521-12732-5 Full Contact 3B with Self-study CD-ROM
ISBN 978-0-521-12747-9 Teacher's Edition 3 with Assessment Audio CD / CD-ROM
ISBN 978-0-521-12743-1 Class Audio CDs 3
ISBN 978-0-521-12712-7 Classware 3
ISBN 978-0-521-12740-0 DVD 3

For a full list of components, visit www.cambridge.org/fourcorners

Art direction, book design, photo research, and layout services: Adventure House, NYC
Audio production: CityVox, NYC
Video production: Steadman Productions

Authors' acknowledgments

Many people contributed to the development of *Four Corners*. The authors and publisher would like to particularly thank the following **reviewers**:

Nele Noe, **Academy for Educational Development, Qatar Independent Secondary School for Girls**, Doha, Qatar; Yuan-hsun Chuang, **Soo Chow University**, Taipei, Taiwan; Celso Frade and Sonia Maria Baccari de Godoy, **Associaçao Alumni**, São Paulo, Brazil; Pablo Stucchi, **Antonio Raimondi School** and **Instituto San Ignacio de Loyola**, Lima, Peru; Kari Miller, **Binational Center**, Quito, Ecuador; Alex K. Oliveira, **Boston University**, Boston, MA, USA; Elisabeth Blom, **Casa Thomas Jefferson**, Brasilia, Brazil; Henry Grant, **CCBEU – Campinas**, Campinas, Brazil; Maria do Rosário, **CCBEU – Franca**, Franca, Brazil; Ane Cibele Palma, **CCBEU Inter Americano**, Curitiba, Brazil; Elen Flavia Penques da Costa, **Centro de Cultura Idiomas – Taubate**, Taubate, Brazil; Inara Lúcia Castillo Couto, **CEL LEP – São Paulo**, São Paulo, Brazil; Geysa de Azevedo Moreira, **Centro Cultural Brasil Estados Unidos (CCBEU Belém)**, Belém, Brazil; Sonia Patricia Cardoso, **Centro de Idiomas Universidad Manuela Beltrán**, Barrio Cedritos, Colombia; Geraldine Itiago Losada, **Centro Universitario Grupo Sol (Musali)**, Mexico City, Mexico; Nick Hilmers, **DePaul University**, Chicago, IL, USA; Monica L. Montemayor Menchaca, **EDIMSA**, Metepec, Mexico; Angela Whitby, **Edu-Idiomas Language School**, Cholula, Puebla, Mexico; Mary Segovia, **El Monte Rosemead Adult School**, Rosemead, CA, USA; Dr. Deborah Aldred, **ELS Language Centers, Middle East Region**, Abu Dhabi, United Arab Emirates; Leslie Lott, **Embassy CES**, Ft. Lauderdale, FL, USA; M. Martha Lengeling, **Escuela de Idiomas**, Guanajuato, Mexico; Pablo Frias, **Escuela de Idiomas UNAPEC**, Santo Domingo, Dominican Republic; Tracy Vanderhoek, **ESL Language Center**, Toronto, Canada; Kris Vicca and Michael McCollister, **Feng Chia University**, Taichung, Taiwan; Flávia Patricia do Nascimento Martins, **First Idiomas**, Sorocaba, Brazil; Andrea Taylor, **Florida State University in Panama**, Panamá, Panama; Carlos Lizárraga González, **Groupo Educativo Angloamericano**, Mexico City, Mexico; Dr. Martin Endley, **Hanyang University**, Seoul, Korea; Mauro Luiz Pinheiro, **IBEU Ceará**, Ceará, Brazil; Ana Lúcia da Costa Maia de Almeida, **IBEU Copacabana**, Copacabana, Brazil; Ana Lucia Almeida, Elisa Borges, **IBEU Rio**, Rio de Janeiro, Brazil; Maristela Silva, **ICBEU Manaus**, Manaus, Brazil; Magaly Mendes Lemos, **ICBEU São José dos Campos**, São José dos Campos, Brazil; Augusto Pelligrini Filho, **ICBEU São Luis**, São Luis, Brazil; Leonardo Mercado, **ICPNA**, Lima, Peru; Lucia Rangel Lugo, **Instituto Tecnológico de San Luis Potosí**, San Luis Potosí, Mexico; Maria Guadalupe Hernández Lozada, **Instituto Tecnológico de Tlalnepantla**, Tlalnepantla de Baz, Mexico; Greg Jankunis, **International Education Service**, Tokyo, Japan; Karen Stewart, **International House Veracruz**, Veracruz, Mexico; George Truscott, **Kinki University**, Osaka, Japan; Bo-Kyung Lee, **Hankuk University of Foreign Studies**, Seoul, Korea; Andy Burki, **Korea University, International Foreign Language School**, Seoul, Korea; Jinseo Noh, **Kwangwoon University**, Seoul, Korea; Nadezhda Nazarenko, **Lone Star College**, Houston, TX, USA; Carolyn Ho, **Lone Star College-Cy-Fair**, Cypress, TX, USA; Alice Ya-fen Chou, **National Taiwan University of Science and Technology**, Taipei, Taiwan; Gregory Hadley, **Niigata University of International and Information Studies, Department of Information Culture**, Niigata-shi, Japan; Raymond Dreyer, **Northern Essex Community College**, Lawrence, MA, USA; Mary Keter Terzian Megale, **One Way Línguas-Suzano**, São Paulo, Brazil; Jason Moser, **Osaka Shoin Joshi University**, Kashiba-shi, Japan; Bonnie Cheeseman, **Pasadena Community College** and **UCLA American Language Center**, Los Angeles, CA, USA; Simon Banha, **Phil Young's English School**, Curitiba, Brazil; Oh Jun Il, **Pukyong National University**, Busan, Korea; Carmen Gehrke, **Quatrum English Schools**, Porto Alegre, Brazil; Atsuko K. Yamazaki, **Shibaura Institute of Technology**, Saitama, Japan; Wen hsiang Su, **Shi Chien University, Kaohsiung Campus**, Kaohsiung, Taiwan; Richmond Stroupe, **Soka University, World Language Center**, Hachioji, Tokyo, Japan; Lynne Kim, **Sun Moon University (Institute for Language Education)**, Cheon An City, Chung Nam, Korea; Hiroko Nishikage, **Taisho University**, Tokyo, Japan; Diaña Peña Munoz and Zaira Kuri, **The Anglo**, Mexico City, Mexico; Alistair Campbell, **Tokyo University of Technology**, Tokyo, Japan; Song-won Kim, **TTI (Teacher's Training Institute)**, Seoul, Korea; Nancy Alarcón, **UNAM FES Zaragoza Language Center**, Mexico City, Mexico; Laura Emilia Fierro López, **Universidad Autónoma de Baja California**, Mexicali, Mexico; María del Rocío Domíngeuz Gaona, **Universidad Autónoma de Baja California**, Tijuana, Mexico; Saul Santos Garcia, **Universidad Autónoma de Nayarit**, Nayarit, Mexico; Christian Meléndez, **Universidad Católica de El Salvador**, San Salvador, El Salvador; Irasema Mora Pablo, **Universidad de Guanajuato**, Guanajuato, Mexico; Alberto Peto, **Universidad de Oxaca**, Tehuantepec, Mexico; Carolina Rodriguez Beltan, **Universidad Manuela Beltrán, Centro Colombo Americano**, and **Universidad Jorge Tadeo Lozano**, Bogotá, Colombia; Nidia Milena Molina Rodriguez, **Universidad Manuela Beltrán** and **Universidad Militar Nueva Granada**, Bogotá, Colombia; Yolima Perez Arias, **Universidad Nacional de Colombia**, Bogota, Colombia; Héctor Vázquez García, **Universidad Nacional Autónoma de Mexico**, Mexico City, Mexico; Pilar Barrera, **Universidad Técnica de Ambato**, Ambato, Ecuador; Deborah Hulston, **University of Regina**, Regina, Canada; Rebecca J. Shelton, **Valparaiso University, Interlink Language Center**, Valparaiso, IN, USA; Tae Lee, **Yonsei University**, Seodaemun-gu, Seoul, Korea; Claudia Thereza Nascimento Mendes, **York Language Institute**, Rio de Janeiro, Brazil; Jamila Jenny Hakam, **ELT Consultant**, Muscat, Oman; Stephanie Smith, **ELT Consultant**, Austin, TX, USA.

The authors would also like to thank the Four Corners editorial, production, and new media teams, as well as the Cambridge University Press staff and advisors around the world for their contributions and tireless commitment to quality.

Scope and sequence

LEVEL 3A	Learning outcomes	Grammar	Vocabulary
Classroom language Page 2			
Unit 1 Pages 3–12			
Education **A** *I'm taking six classes.* **B** *You're not allowed to . . .* **C** *My behavior* **D** *Alternative education*	**Students can . . .** ☑ ask and talk about routines ☑ express prohibition and obligation ☑ ask and talk about feelings and reactions ☑ discuss advantages and disadvantages	Simple present vs. present continuous Zero conditional	School subjects Feelings and emotions
Unit 2 Pages 13–22			

Personal stories
A *What were you doing?*
B *Guess what!*
 	
C *I was really frightened!*
D *How embarrassing!*
	Students can . . .
	☑ describe what was happening in the past
	☑ announce news
	☑ close a conversation
	☑ tell personal stories
	☑ describe embarrassing moments
		Past continuous vs.
		  simple past
		Participial adjectives
			Sentence adverbs
			Verbs to describe
			  reactions

Unit 3 Pages 23–32			
Style and fashion **A** *Fashion trends* **B** *Does this come in . . . ?* **C** *The latest look* **D** *Views on fashion*	**Students can . . .** ☑ ask about and describe past fashions ☑ ask where something is in a store ☑ ask for a specific product ☑ express opinions about style and fashion ☑ ask and talk about current fashions	*Used to* Defining relative clauses	Fashion statements Clothing styles
Unit 4 Pages 33–42			
Interesting lives **A** *Have you ever been on TV?* **B** *What I mean is, . . .* **C** *Life experiences* **D** *What a life!*	**Students can . . .** ☑ ask and talk about life experiences ☑ check and clarify meaning ☑ describe details of their experiences ☑ ask and talk about a memorable experience	Present perfect Present perfect vs. simple past	Experiences Fun things to do
Unit 5 Pages 43–52			
Our world **A** *Older, taller, and more famous* **B** *I don't believe it!* **C** *World geography* **D** *Natural wonders*	**Students can . . .** ☑ compare human-made structures ☑ express disbelief ☑ say that they don't know something ☑ ask and talk about geographical features ☑ describe natural wonders in their country	Comparatives *Not as . . . as* Superlatives	Human-made wonders Geographical features
Unit 6 Pages 53–62			

Organizing your time
A *A busy week*
B *Can I take a message?*
 	
C *Can you do me a favor?*
D *Time management*
	Students can . . .
	☑ ask and talk about weekend plans
	☑ offer to take a message
	☑ leave a message
	☑ make requests, promises, and offers
	☑ discuss ways to manage time effectively
		Present tenses used for
		  future
		Requests
		Promises and offers with
		  will
			Commitments
			Favors

Functional language	Listening and Pronunciation	Reading and Writing	Speaking
Interactions: Expressing prohibition Expressing obligation	**Listening:** Office rules An interview about homeschooling **Pronunciation:** Stress and rhythm	**Reading:** "Homeschooling" A magazine article **Writing:** Advantages and disadvantages of distance education	• Information exchange about school and work • *Keep talking:* "Find someone who" activity about everyday activities • List of class rules • Information exchange about personal behavior • *Keep talking:* Comparison of behaviors • Discussion about distance education
Interactions: Announcing news Closing a conversation	**Listening:** News about other people A camping trip **Pronunciation:** Intonation in complex sentences	**Reading** "Embarrassing Experiences" An article **Writing:** An embarrassing moment	• Group story about a past event • *Keep talking:* Description of simultaneous past actions • Celebrity news • Personal stories and anecdotes • *Keep talking:* Picture stories • Descriptions of embarrassing moments
Interactions: Asking where things are Asking for an alternative	**Listening:** Clothing purchases An interview with a fashion designer **Pronunciation:** *Used to* and *use to*	**Reading:** "Favorite Fashions" A survey **Writing:** Class survey	• Interview about style and fashion • *Keep talking:* Comparison of two people's past and present styles • Role play of a shopping situation • Opinions on fashion and style • *Keep talking:* Interview about what's hot • Class survey about style and fashion
Interactions: Checking meaning Clarifying meaning	**Listening:** Unusual habits An interview with a grandmother **Pronunciation:** Contrastive stress in responses	**Reading:** "The Life of an Astronaut" An interview **Writing:** Interesting people, places, or things	• Interviews about experiences • *Keep talking:* Information exchange about experiences never had • Information exchange about unusual habits • True and false information about life experiences • *Keep talking:* "Find someone who" activity about everyday experiences • Description of an interesting person or place
Interactions: Expressing disbelief Saying you don't know	**Listening:** An interesting city The Great Barrier Reef **Pronunciation:** Intonation in tag questions	**Reading:** "Seven Wonders of the Natural World" An article **Writing:** A natural wonder	• Comparison of different places • *Keep talking:* Information gap activity about impressive places • Information exchange about human-made structures • Discussion about experiences in different places • *Keep talking:* Advice for foreign visitors • List of the most wonderful places in the country
Interactions: Offering to take a message Leaving a message	**Listening:** Weekend plans Phone messages **Pronunciation:** Reduction of *could you* and *would you*	**Reading:** "How to Manage Your Time" An article **Writing:** Tips for success	• "Find someone who" activity about weekend plans • *Keep talking:* Information exchange about upcoming plans • Role play with phone messages • Class favors, offers, and promises • *Keep talking:* Role play with requests • Quiz about overdoing things

Classroom language

A 🔊 Complete the conversations with the correct sentences. Then listen and check your answers.

What page are we on? ✓Excuse me. I'm very sorry I'm late.
Can you repeat that, please? May I go to the restroom, please?
What's our homework? Which role do you want to play?

A: _Excuse me. I'm very sorry I'm late._

B: That's OK. Next time try to arrive on time.

A: _____

B: Thirteen. We're doing the Warm-up for Unit 2.

A: _____

B: Yes. I said, "Please work with a partner."

A: _____

B: I'll be Student A. You can be Student B.

A: _____

B: No problem. Please try to be quick.

A: _____

B: Please complete the activities for Unit 2 in your workbook.

B Pair work Practice the conversations.

Education

Warm-up

A Describe the pictures. What do you see? What are the students doing?

B How are the classrooms similar or different from your own classroom experiences?

A I'm taking six classes.

1 Vocabulary School subjects

A 🔊 Match the words and the pictures. Then listen and check your answers.

a. algebra
b. art
c. biology
d. chemistry
e. geometry
f. history
g. music
✓ h. physics
i. world geography

1. [h]
2. [ ]
3. [ ]
4. [ ]
5. [ ]
6. [ ]
7. [ ]
8. [ ]
9. [ ]

B 🔊 Complete the chart with the correct school subjects. Then listen and check your answers.

Arts	Math	Science	Social studies
art			

C Pair work Which school subjects are or were easy for you? Which are or were difficult? Tell your partner.

"History and music were easy subjects for me, but algebra was difficult!"

2 Language in context Busy schedules

A 🔊 Listen to three people talk about their schedules. Who doesn't have a job?

I'm a high school student. I love history and world geography. I have a part-time job, too. My parents own a restaurant, so I work there on Saturdays. I guess I'm pretty busy.　– Kenji

I'm a full-time student. I want to be a doctor. I'm taking six classes and preparing for my medical school entrance exams. I study biology and chemistry every night.　– Jan

I'm really busy! I work full-time at a bank. I'm also taking an English class at night with my friend Ricardo. Actually, I'm going to class now. I think I'm late!　– Amelia

B What about you? Do you have a busy schedule? What do you do in a typical week?

3 Grammar 🔊 Simple present vs. present continuous

Use the simple present to describe routines and permanent situations.

Kenji **works** on Saturdays.

Jan **studies** every night.

Kenji's parents **own** a restaurant.

Use the present continuous to describe actions in progress or temporary situations.

Amelia **is going** to class right now.

Jan **is preparing** for her medical school entrance exams.

Amelia and Ricardo **are taking** an English class together.

Verbs not usually used in continuous tenses	
believe	mean
have	own
hope	remember
know	seem
like	understand
love	want

A Complete the conversations with the simple present or present continuous forms of the verbs. Then practice with a partner.

1. **A:** _____*Are*_____ you ____*taking*____ (take) a lot of classes these days?

   B: I _____ (take) just two: world geography and physics. I _____ (have) a full-time job, so I _____ (not / have) a lot of free time.

2. **A:** How often _____ you _____ (go) to the library?

   B: I _____ (go) every Saturday. But I _____ (study) at home a lot, too. I _____ (prepare) for an important exam.

3. **A:** How _____ (be) your English class?

   B: It _____ (be) fine. I _____ (like) English and _____ (want) to improve my speaking. But we _____ (be) only in the first lesson!

4. **A:** What _____ the teacher _____ (do) now?

   B: She _____ (help) some students. They _____ (ask) her questions. They _____ (seem) confused about something.

B Pair work Ask and answer the questions in Part A. Answer with your own information.

4 Speaking School and work

A Pair work Read the list. Add one set of questions about school or work. Then ask and answer the questions with a partner.

- What's your favorite class? Are you learning anything interesting?
- Do you have a job? If so, what do you do?
- Are you studying for any exams? Do you study alone or with others?
- What job do you want someday? Are you doing anything to prepare for it?
- Why are you studying English? What do you hope to do in this class?
- _____ ? _____ ?

B Group work Share any interesting information from Part A.

5 Keep talking!

Go to page 123 for more practice.

I can ask and talk about routines.

1 Interactions — Prohibition and obligation

A Do you always follow rules? Do you ever break rules? If so, when?

B ◀)) Listen to the conversation. What *can* students do in the class? Then practice the conversation.

Justin: Excuse me. Do you mind if I sit here?

Fei: Not at all. Go ahead.

Justin: Thanks. I'm Justin, by the way.

Fei: Hi. I'm Fei. Are you new in this class?

Justin: Yeah. Today is my first day. Hey, can we drink coffee in class?

Fei: No. You can't eat or drink in class. It's one of the rules.

Justin: Really? Good to know.

Fei: Oh, and there's another rule. You have to turn off your cell phone.

Justin: OK. Thanks for letting me know.

Fei: Sure. Do you want to be my language partner today? We can choose our speaking partners in this class.

Justin: OK. Thanks.

C ◀)) Read the expressions below. Complete each box with a similar expression from the conversation. Then listen and check your answers.

Expressing prohibition

You can't . . .
You're not allowed to . . .
You're not permitted to . . .

Expressing obligation

_____
You need to . . .
You must . . .

D **Pair work** Look at the common signs. Say the rules. Take turns.

"You're not permitted to use cell phones."

2 Listening First day at work

A 🔊 Listen to Joel's co-workers explain the office rules on his first day at work.
Number the pictures from 1 to 6.

B 🔊 Listen again. Write the office rules.

1. _____   4. _____
2. _____   5. _____
3. _____   6. _____

3 Speaking Class rules

A Pair work Make a list of five important rules for your class like the one below.

Class rules

1. You must raise your hand to speak.

2. You can't send or read text messages.

3. You have to turn off your cell phone.

4. You're not permitted to chew gum.

5. You're allowed to sit anywhere you want.

B Group work Compare your list with another pair. Choose the five most important rules.

C Class activity Share your lists. Can you and your teacher agree on a list of class rules?

I can express prohibition and obligation.

C My behavior

1 Vocabulary Feelings and emotions

A 🔊 Match the words and the pictures. Then listen and check your answers.

a. angry	c. hungry	e. lonely	g. scared	i. thirsty
b. busy	d. jealous	f. nervous	h. sleepy	j. upset

B Pair work Why do you think the people in the pictures feel the way they do? Discuss your ideas.

2 Conversation Feeling nervous

A 🔊 Listen to the conversation. Why is Nate eating so late?

Nate: Hello?

Laura: Hi, Nate. It's Laura. Are you busy?

Nate: Not really. I'm just eating some ice cream.

Laura: Really? Why are you eating so late?

Nate: Oh, I have an exam tomorrow, and I'm kind of nervous about it. I eat when I'm nervous. I'm not even hungry! It's not good, I know.

Laura: Well, a lot of people eat when they're nervous. If I'm nervous about something, I just try not to think about it.

Nate: That's easier said than done! But what do you do if you have a really important exam?

Laura: I study a lot, of course!

B 🔊 Listen to the rest of the conversation. Why did Laura call Nate?

8

3 Grammar 🔊 **Zero conditional**

Zero conditional sentences describe things that are generally true. Use the simple present for both the if *clause (the condition) and the main clause.*

What **do** you **do** if you **have** a really important exam?
    If I **have** a really important exam, I **study** a lot.
    I **study** a lot if I **have** a really important exam.

You can usually substitute when *for* if *in zero conditional sentences.*
If I'm nervous about something, I just try not to think about it.
When I'm nervous about something, I just try not to think about it.

A Match the conditions and the main clauses. Then compare with a partner.

1. If I'm nervous before an exam, _____
2. When I'm busy with chores at home, _____
3. If I wake up and feel hungry, _____
4. When I get angry at someone, _____
5. If my friends don't call me for a few days, _____
6. When I feel sleepy on Sunday mornings, _____

a. I ask a family member to do some.
b. I start to get lonely.
c. I have something healthy, like an apple.
d. I usually don't say anything to him or her.
e. I like to stay in bed.
f. I take a deep breath and try to relax.

B Pair work Make true sentences about your behavior with the conditions in Part A. Tell your partner.

"If I'm nervous before an exam, I study with a friend."

4 Pronunciation Stress and rhythm

A 🔊 Listen and repeat. Notice how stressed words occur with a regular rhythm.

When I'm **lonely**, I **like** to **chat** or **talk** on the **phone** with my **friends**.

B Pair work Practice the sentences from Exercise 3A. Pay attention to your stress and rhythm.

5 Speaking Different behaviors

Group work Read the list. Add two more questions with *if* or *when*.
Then ask and answer them.

* How do you feel when you're home alone at night?
* What do you do when you get jealous?
* What do you do if you feel sleepy in class?
* How do you feel when you speak English in class?
* _____
* _____

6 Keep talking!

Go to page **124** for more practice.

I can ask and talk about feelings and reactions. ☑

D Alternative education

1 Reading ◄))

A What is homeschooling? Do you know any homeschooled students?

B Read the article. What is a "curriculum," and who chooses it for homeschooled students?

Homeschooling

Homeschooling is a choice made by some parents to provide education to their children in their own homes. It's popular in the United States, and it is becoming more popular in the United Kingdom, Australia, South Africa, and Japan.

There are several advantages to homeschooling. For example, parents choose what their children learn. Because parents can teach their children one on one, they often understand the curriculum better and more quickly, too. On the other hand, if their children need more time to learn something, parents can work with them at a slower pace. Parents also like to spend more time together as a family, and children feel safe at home. A safe environment often leads to better learning.

There are disadvantages as well. Homeschooled students often feel lonely because they don't spend as much time with other kids their age. They don't get to talk with classmates about things like parents and homework. Parents also feel lonely because they must spend time teaching children and don't get to talk with other adults at work. In addition, homeschooled students sometimes cannot play school sports or participate in other activities and programs available to people in a school.

Only you can decide if homeschooling is right for you and your family. Take the time to do the research and consider the pros and cons.

Source: www.wisegeek.com/what-is-home-schooling.htm

American Parents' Reasons for Homeschooling

Better education at home	48.9%	Disagree with school's curriculum	12.1%
Religious reasons	38.4%	School is too easy	11.6%
Poor learning environment at school	25.6%	No schools nearby	11.5%
Family reasons	16.8%	Child's behavior problems	9.0%
To develop child's character	15.1%	Child's special needs	8.2%

Source: nces.ed.gov/pubs2001/Homeschool/reasons.asp

C Read the article again. Complete the chart with at least three advantages and three disadvantages of homeschooling.

Advantages of homeschooling (+)	Disadvantages of homeschooling (−)
parents choose the curriculum	*kids can feel lonely*

D Pair work Do you think you and your family would like homeschooling? Why or why not? Tell your partner.

2 Listening Is homeschooling for you?

A 🔊 Listen to Julie and her parents discuss homeschooling. What do they like about it, and what are their challenges? Check (✓) the correct answers.

	Likes	Challenges	Advice
Julie	☐ the classroom ☐ the hours ☐ the teachers	☐ texting friends ☐ not seeing friends in class ☐ being in a real school	
Julie's parents	☐ teaching together ☐ choosing the curriculum ☐ working at home	☐ scheduling ☐ giving grades ☐ knowing every subject	

B 🔊 Listen again. What advice do Julie and her parents give to people considering homeschooling? Complete the chart with their advice.

3 Writing Distance education

A Pair work Read the definition of distance education. Then make a list of its advantages and disadvantages.

Distance education is a type of education where students work on their own at home and communicate with teachers and other students using email, message boards, instant messaging, chat rooms, and other forms of computer-based communication.

B Do you think learning English by distance education is a good idea or a bad idea? Write a paragraph to explain your opinion. Use the model and your list from Part A.

Advantages of Distance Education
I think learning English by distance education is a very
good idea. There are many advantages. For example, students
can work at their own speed. This is good for people with full-
time jobs or people who can't go to regular classes . . .

C Pair work Compare your ideas.

4 Speaking Advantages and disadvantages

A Group work What are the advantages and disadvantages of these types of learning? Discuss your ideas.

large classes	private lessons with a tutor	studying abroad
small classes	online learning	watching movies in English

B Class activity How do you prefer to learn? What type of learning is the most popular?

> *I can* discuss advantages and disadvantages. ☑

Wrap-up

1 Quick pair review

Lesson A Do you remember? Cross out the word that doesn't belong.
Then write the category. You have two minutes.

1. ____math____   algebra   ~~history~~   geometry
2. _____   art   history   world geography
3. _____   music   art   algebra
4. _____   biology   geometry   chemistry

Lesson B Guess! Think of a place that has rules. Tell your partner things
you can and can't do there, but don't say the name of the place. Can your partner
guess it? You have two minutes.

A: *You're not permitted to talk. You must turn off your cell phone.*
B: *Is it a library?*

Lesson C Find out! What is one thing both you and your partner do in
each situation? You have three minutes.

- What do you do if you feel scared?
- What do you do if you get a phone call in class?
- What do you do if you have a lot of homework?

A: *If I'm scared, I turn on the lights. Do you?*
B: *No. I lock the doors if I'm scared. Do you?*
A: *Yes.*

Lesson D Give your opinion! What are two advantages and two
disadvantages of taking a class online? You have three minutes.

2 In the real world

What is a multi-age classroom? Go online and find information in English
about one. Then write about it.

- What ages or grades are in the classroom?
- What are some advantages?
- What are some disadvantages?

> *A Multi-Age Classroom*
> At Ambuehl Elementary School, first-, second-, and
> third-graders are in the same classroom. One advantage
> is that younger students learn from older students.
> Another advantage is that . . .

Personal stories

Warm-up

A Look at the pictures. Which story would you like to hear? Rank them from 1 (very much) to 6 (not much).

B Do you prefer to tell stories about yourself or hear stories about other people? Why?

A *What were you doing?*

1 Vocabulary Sentence adverbs

A 🔊 Match the pictures and the sentences. Then listen and check your answers.

1.   2.   3.   4.

_____ **Amazingly**, she came home last night.   _____ **Sadly**, my cat disappeared last year.

_____ **Fortunately**, she was very healthy.   _____ **Strangely**, she had on a little sweater.

5.   6.   7.   8.

_____ **Luckily**, someone found it.   _____ **Surprisingly**, she brought it to my home.

_____ **Suddenly**, I realized I didn't have it.   _____ **Unfortunately**, I lost my wallet yesterday.

B Pair work Use sentence adverbs to describe incidents that happened to you or people you know. Tell your partner.

"Amazingly, my brother passed his physics exam last week. He didn't study at all!"

2 Language in context Lights out!

A 🔊 Listen to two people describe what they were doing when the power went out last night. What did they do after the power went out?

I was cooking pasta when suddenly everything went dark. Luckily, I had some candles. I couldn't finish making my meal, so I just ate cereal for dinner.

– *Angela*

While my friends and I were watching a movie at home, the lights went out. Unfortunately, no one knew how the movie ended. So, we took turns telling our own endings.

– *Tetsu*

B What about you? Have you ever been in a blackout? What did you do?

14

3 Grammar ◄)) **Past continuous vs. simple past**

Use the past continuous to describe an action in progress in the past.

Angela **was cooking** pasta last night.   Tetsu and his friends **were watching** a movie.

Use the simple past for an event that interrupts that action in progress.

Angela **was cooking** pasta when everything **went** dark.

While Tetsu and his friends **were watching** a movie, the lights **went** out.

A Complete the conversations with the past continuous or simple past forms of the verbs. Then practice with a partner.

1. **A:** What ____*were*____ you ____*doing*____
    (do) last night when the storm
    _____ (begin)?
   B: I _____ (use) my computer.
    While I _____ (write) my report,
    the electricity suddenly _____
    (go) off.
   A: _____ you _____
    (lose) your work?
   B: Yeah. Unfortunately, I _____
    (need) to do it again.

2. **A:** How _____ you
    _____ (break) your foot?
   B: Oh, I _____ (ski).
   A: Really? _____ it
    _____ (hurt)?
   B: Of course! But fortunately, someone
    _____ (call) an ambulance.
   A: That's good.
   B: Yeah, and while I _____ (wait),
    my friends _____ (bring) me
    hot chocolate.

B Pair work Ask and answer questions about what you were doing at the times below.

7:00 this morning   10:00 last night   4:30 yesterday afternoon   this time yesterday

4 Pronunciation Intonation in complex sentences

◄)) Listen and repeat. Notice how each clause has its own intonation pattern.

Angela was cooking pasta when everything went dark.

When everything went dark, Angela was cooking pasta.

5 Speaking Story time

Group work Complete a sentence below with your own idea. Your group adds sentences with adverbs to create a story. Take turns.

- I was talking to my best friend when . . .
- I was sleeping one night when . . .
- I was walking down the street when . . .
- I was checking my messages when . . .

A: *I was talking to my best friend when my phone rang.*
B: *Strangely, it was a phone number I didn't know.*
C: *Luckily, I answered the phone, because it was . . .*

6 Keep talking!

Go to page 125 for more practice.

Go to page 125 for more practice.

I can describe what was happening in the past. ☑

1 Interactions · Sharing news

A Think about different people you know. Do you have any news about them?

B 🔊 Listen to the conversation. What news is Diana sharing?
Then practice the conversation.

> **Ruben:** Hi, Diana. How are you?
> **Diana:** I'm fine. Guess what!
> **Ruben:** What?
> **Diana:** Do you remember Joe from our photography class?
> **Ruben:** Joe? Oh, yeah. Is he OK?
> **Diana:** Oh, he's fine. It's just that he got into film school in Los Angeles. He's wants to be a director.
> **Ruben:** Really? Good for him.
> **Diana:** Yeah. I hear he really likes it.
> **Ruben:** That's fantastic!
> **Diana:** Yeah. Hey, I need to get going. I'm late for work.
> **Ruben:** Oh, OK. I'll call you later.

C 🔊 Read the expressions below. Complete each box with a similar expression from the conversation. Then listen and check your answers.

Announcing news	Closing a conversation
_____	_____
Did you hear what happened?	Listen, I've got to run.
You'll never guess what happened!	Sorry, I have to go.

D Pair work Have conversations like the one in Part B. Use these ideas.

Your classmate Lucy Kim moved away. She moved to Spain to study art.

Your teacher Bill Jones got married. He married his girlfriend from high school.

Your friend Pedro Garcia was on TV. He was on a game show and won!

2 Listening You'll never guess!

A  Listen to Michael and Wendy talk about four different people they know. Number the people from 1 to 4 in the order they talk about them. There is one extra person.

☐ a classmate   ☐ a co-worker   ☐ a family member   ☐ a neighbor   ☐ a teacher

B Listen again. Check (✓) the true sentences. Correct the false ones.

1. ☐ Greg is graduating from middle school.
2. ☐ Eva bought a brand-new red car.
3. ☐ Mr. Landers is going to teach a new class.
4. ☐ Cathy is going to be in the school play.

3 Speaking Celebrity news

A Pair work Think of four famous people. What is some interesting news about them? Complete the chart.

	Famous person	News
1.		
2.		
3.		
4.		

B Class activity Announce your news about the famous people to a classmate. Then close the conversation and talk to another classmate.

C Class activity Who heard the most interesting news?

> I can announce news. ☑
> I can close a conversation. ☑

C I was really frightened!

1 Vocabulary Verbs to describe reactions

A ◀)) Match the words and the pictures. Then listen and check your answers.

a. amuse	c. confuse	e. embarrass	g. frighten
b. challenge	d. disgust	f. excite	h. interest

 1. ☐
 2. ☐
 3. ☐
 4. ☐

 5. ☐
 6. ☐
 7. ☐
 8. ☐

B Pair work What amuses you? challenges you? confuses you? etc.
Tell your partner.

2 Conversation Around the campfire

A ◀)) Listen to the conversation. What frightened Paul?

David: . . . and that's what was on the floor!

Jim: Yuck! That story was disgusting!

Paul: Well, listen to this. I was watching a movie at home one night when I heard a strange noise outside the window.

David: What did you do?

Paul: I was really frightened! I was watching a horror movie, *and* I was sitting in the dark. Anyway, I walked to the window, opened the curtains, and saw a face!

Jim: No way! That's frightening!

Paul: Not really. It was just my roommate.

David: Your roommate?

Paul: Yeah. Unfortunately, he lost his key and couldn't get in the house. He was really embarrassed!

B ◀)) Listen to the rest of the conversation.
How did Paul's roommate react?

3 Grammar ◁)) Participial adjectives

Use present participles (-ing) to describe someone or something that causes a reaction.	*Use past participles (-ed) to describe a person's reaction to someone or something.*
That story was **disgusting**.	I was **disgusted** by that story.
The noise was really **frightening**.	I was really **frightened** by the noise.
His actions were really **embarrassing**.	He was really **embarrassed**.

Circle the correct words. Then compare with a partner.

1. This short story is very (challenging) / **challenged**. There's a lot of difficult vocabulary.
2. I'm really **exciting** / **excited** to hear about your trip. Tell me all about it!
3. I liked your story, but I'm **confusing** / **confused** by the ending. Can you explain it?
4. I think my neighbor's stories about her life are very **amusing** / **amused**.
5. I never feel **frightening** / **frightened** when people tell me ghost stories.
6. That joke wasn't funny at all. It was **disgusting** / **disgusted**.
7. That movie was **boring** / **bored**. It wasn't **interesting** / **interested** at all.
8. I'm **surprising** / **surprised** you were **embarrassing** / **embarrassed** by my story.

4 Listening Is that really true?

A ◁)) Listen to Mark's story. Check (✓) the two adjectives that best describe it.

☐ challenging   ☐ frightening   ☐ disgusting   ☐ amusing

B ◁)) Listen again. Answer the questions.

1. What were Mark and his friend doing in the tent? _____
2. What did they first hear outside the tent? _____
3. What did Mark's friend want to do? _____
4. What did the voice outside the tent say? _____

5 Speaking My own experience

A Think about your own experiences. Choose one of the topics from the list below. Then take notes to prepare to talk about it.

an exciting day	a frightening experience
a confusing moment	an amusing situation
a challenging situation	an interesting conversation

B Pair work Tell your partner about your experience. Ask and answer questions for more information.

6 Keep talking!

Go to page 126 for more practice.

I can tell personal stories. ☑

D How embarrassing!

1 Reading 🔊

A How do you react when you feel embarrassed? Do you turn red? Do you get angry if people laugh at you?

B Read the article. Where did each person's embarrassing moment happen?

Home	Metro	Sports	Opinions	Arts	Photos	Videos	Search

Embarrassing Experiences

By Jack Preston

Last week, *Student Times* reporter Jack Preston asked students, "What's the most embarrassing experience you've ever had?" Here are five of his favorite responses.

This happened at work a few years ago. I was on an elevator, and a man got on that I didn't know. He asked, "How are you?" I answered, "Pretty good." Then he asked, "What's new?" and I said, "Nothing much." Finally, he turned and said, "Do you mind?" He was on his cell phone! I was so embarrassed! ☐ – *Susan*

I sing all the time. One time, a few years ago, I was singing in the shower when my sister came into the bathroom and recorded me! Later, we were driving, and my sister put on some music. ☐ It was me! I was really embarrassed and turned bright red. – *Becky*

I fell asleep in math class once. I closed my eyes for a second, and the next thing I remember is my teacher's voice. He was asking me a question. When I didn't answer, he walked over to my desk. He asked the question again. ☐ – *Alex*

My friend's parents had a birthday party for her at their new house last year. They had these glass doors that went out to the backyard. We were all outside, and I had to use the restroom. So I was running to the house and then – BAM! I hit the glass doors. I was really confused for a minute. I thought they were open, but they were closed! ☐ – *Anita*

When I was in middle school, I bought this cool new sweater. I wore it to a school dance the next evening, and everyone laughed at me when I came in. The sweater was inside out! So I went into the restroom to change and came back out. ☐ Everyone laughed at me again. – *Evan*

C Read the article again. Write the numbers of the missing sentences in the correct paragraphs.

1. Luckily, I knew the answer.
2. Fortunately, the doors opened, and I got off.
3. Unfortunately, it was now on backwards!
4. Suddenly, she started to laugh.
5. Amazingly, I wasn't hurt at all.

D Pair work Whose story do you think is the most embarrassing? Discuss your ideas.

2 Writing An embarrassing moment

A Think of an embarrassing moment that happened to you or someone you know. Answer the questions.

- When did it happen? _____
- Where did it happen? _____
- Who was there? _____
- Why was it embarrassing? _____

B Write a description of an embarrassing moment that happened to you or someone you know. Use the model and your answers in Part A to help you.

> *Embarrassed at the Supermarket*
> *When I was about six years old, I was at the supermarket with my mom. She was shopping for groceries. I wanted some candy, but my mom didn't want to buy me any. So, when my mother wasn't looking, I took some candy and put it into the cart. The problem was that I put the candy into the wrong cart. . . .*

C **Class activity** Post your papers around the classroom. Then read the stories and rate them from 1 (very embarrassing) to 4 (not embarrassing). Which stories are the most embarrassing?

3 Speaking It happened to me!

A Imagine you are the person in one of these pictures. Take notes to prepare to tell the story.

B **Group work** Tell your stories. Ask and answer questions for more information.

A: *I was having dinner with a friend. We were eating pizza and drinking soda. Suddenly, I spilled my soda on my clothes.*
B: *Oh, no! What did you do?*

> I can *describe embarrassing moments.* ☑

Wrap-up

1 Quick pair review

Lesson A Brainstorm! Make a list of sentence adverbs. How many do you know? You have one minute.

Lesson B Do you remember? Complete the expressions with the correct words to announce news and close a conversation. You have one minute.

1. Did you hear _____ ?
2. You'll _____ what happened!
3. Guess _____ !
4. Listen, I've _____ run.
5. Hey, I need to _____ .
6. Sorry, I _____ to go.

Lesson C Test your partner! Say four present or past participles. Can your partner use them correctly in a sentence? Take turns. You have two minutes.

A: *Disgusting.*
B: *In my opinion, hamburgers are disgusting!*

Lesson D Find out! What are two things both you and your partner do when you are embarrassed? You have one minute.

A: *When I'm embarrassed, I laugh a lot. Do you?*
B: *No, I don't. I turn red, though. Do you?*
A: *Yes, my cheeks turn red, too!*

2 In the real world

Go online and find an embarrassing, interesting, or amusing story in English about a famous person. Then write about it.

> *Beyoncé's Embarrassing Moment*
> *Beyoncé had an embarrassing experience at a concert. She was walking down the stairs on stage when she tripped and fell. Luckily, she didn't get hurt. Actually she got up and continued to sing! . . .*

Style and fashion

Warm-up

A Describe the picture. What are the people doing?

B Which styles do you like? Which don't you like? Why?

A Fashion trends

1 Vocabulary Fashion statements

A 🔊 Complete the chart with the correct words. Then listen and check your answers.

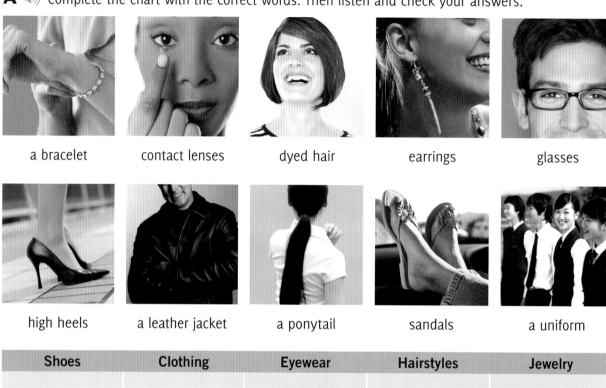

| a bracelet | contact lenses | dyed hair | earrings | glasses |

| high heels | a leather jacket | a ponytail | sandals | a uniform |

Shoes	Clothing	Eyewear	Hairstyles	Jewelry

B **Pair work** Which things in Part A do you wear or have? Tell your partner.

2 Language in context Fashion history

A 🔊 Read about three fashions from the past. Who wore each fashion?

Togas Two thousand years ago, Roman men used to wear sandals and a long piece of clothing called a toga.

Wigs In the seventeenth and eighteenth centuries, rich men and women in England and France used to wear long wigs. Some of the wigs had ponytails.

Leather jackets In the 1950s, many American men used to wear leather jackets with jeans. Before that time, most teenagers didn't use to wear jeans.

B Do people still wear the fashions from Part A today? If so, how are they similar or different?

3 Grammar 🔊 *Used to*

Used to *refers to something that was true in the past but isn't anymore or something that happened regularly in the past but doesn't anymore.*

I **used to** have a black leather jacket.

Men and women in England and France **used to** wear long wigs.

Did you **use to** dye your hair?

    Yes, I **used to** dye my hair all the time, but I don't dye it anymore.

    No, I **didn't use to** dye my hair, but I do now.

A Write sentences with *used to* (✓) or *didn't use to* (✗). Then compare with a partner.

1. Max / (✓) dye his hair black   *Max used to dye his hair black.*
2. Carly / (✗) wear a uniform to school   _____
3. Tina and I / (✓) have ponytails   _____
4. Britney / (✓) wear the same bracelet every day   _____
5. Roberto and Ana / (✗) wear glasses   _____
6. Kendra / (✗) like leather skirts   _____

B Pair work Complete the sentences with true information. Tell your partner.

1. I used to _____ as a kid, but I don't now.
2. I didn't use to _____ , but some of my friends did.
3. Lots of people used to _____ , but they don't now.

4 Pronunciation *Used to* and *use to*

🔊 Listen and repeat. Notice how *used to* and *use to* sound the same.

  /yustə/   /yustə/

I **used to** wear a uniform.   I didn't **use to** dye my hair, but I do now.

5 Speaking Past and present

A Pair work Read the list. Add two more questions about style and fashion. Then interview your partner. Take notes.

* What kind of clothing did you use to wear?
* What kind of hairstyles did you use to have?
* What's something you didn't use to wear but do now?
* _____
* _____

B Pair work Tell another classmate any interesting information about your partner's style and fashion.

6 Keep talking!

Student A go to page **127** and
Student B go to page **128** for more practice.

Student A go to page **127** and
Student B go to page **128** for more practice.

I can ask about and describe past fashions. ☑

1 Interactions   Shopping questions

A Where do you like to shop for clothes? What kinds of clothes do you like?

B 🔊 Listen to the conversations. What size does Jenny want?
Then practice the conversations.

> **Jenny:** Excuse me.
> **Salesclerk 1:** Yes?
> **Jenny:** Where are the raincoats?
> **Salesclerk 1:** They're on the second floor, in Outerwear.
> **Jenny:** Thank you.

> **Jenny:** Excuse me.
> **Salesclerk 2:** Can I help you?
> **Jenny:** Yes. Does this come in a medium?
> **Salesclerk 2:** I believe so. Let's see. . . . Yes, here you go.
> **Jenny:** Thank you.
> **Salesclerk 2:** If you want to try it on, the fitting rooms are over there.

C 🔊 Read the expressions below. Complete each box with a similar expression from the conversations. Then listen and check your answers.

Asking where things are
_____
Where can I find the . . . ?
Could you tell me where the . . . are?

Asking for an alternative
_____
Do you have this in . . . ?
Can I get this in . . . ?

D Pair work Have conversations like the ones in Part B. Use these items.

2 Listening Shopping for clothes

A 🔊 Listen to four customers shopping in a clothing store. Number the items they discuss from 1 to 4. There are two extra items.

☐ ☐ ☐ ☐ ☐ ☐

B 🔊 Listen again. Does each customer ask the salesclerk for the location or an alternative of the item? Write L (location) or A (alternative).

1. ____   2. ____   3. ____   4. ____

3 Speaking In a department store

Group work Role-play the situation. Then change roles.

Student A: You are a salesclerk in a department store. Student B is shopping for a particular item. Direct Student B to the correct section of the store. Use the picture to help you.

Student B: You are shopping in a department store. Students A and C are salesclerks. Ask Student A where a particular clothing item is. Then ask Student C for a different item.

Student C: You are a salesclerk in a department store. Student B is shopping for a particular item in your section of the store. Help Student B get a different item.

A: *Good afternoon. Can I help you?*
B: *Yes. Where can I find women's shoes?*
A: *On the second floor, in Footwear.*

> I can ask where something is in a store. ✓
> I can ask for a specific product. ✓

C The latest look

1 Vocabulary Clothing styles

A 🔊 Write the correct adjectives to describe the clothing. Then listen and check your answers.

fashionable
✓ flashy
glamorous
old-fashioned

1. _____flashy_____
2. _____
3. _____
4. _____

 1
 2
 3
 4

retro
tacky
trendy
✓ weird

5. _____weird_____
6. _____
7. _____
8. _____

 5
 6
 7
 8

B Pair work Which styles do you like? Which don't you like? Why? Tell your partner.

2 Conversation People-watching

A 🔊 Listen to the conversation. What does Ryan think of the man's tie?

Ryan: Look at that woman's jacket!

Jill: Wow! It's pretty flashy. I definitely think she's someone who likes to stand out in a crowd.

Ryan: I know what you mean. I like clothes which don't attract a lot of attention.

Jill: Really?

Ryan: Yeah. I usually shop for clothes that are simple and inexpensive. Hey, check out that guy's tie. Talk about old-fashioned!

Jill: Do you think so? Actually, I think it's pretty fashionable. It's kind of retro.

Ryan: Well, I'd never wear anything like that.

B 🔊 Listen to the rest of the conversation. How does Jill describe her style?

3 Grammar 🔊 **Defining relative clauses**

Defining relative clauses specify which or what kind of people or things you are describing.

Use that *or* who *for people.*

I'm a person **that** loves flashy clothes.

She's someone **who** likes to stand out in a crowd.

Use that *or* which *for things.*

I shop for clothes **that** are simple and inexpensive.

He likes clothes **which** don't attract a lot of attention.

A Complete each sentence with *that, who,* or *which.* Then compare with a partner.

1. I prefer salesclerks _____ are honest with me.
2. I'm the kind of person _____ rarely follows fashion.
3. I hardly ever wear clothes _____ are trendy.
4. I know someone _____ loves expensive clothes.
5. Some of my friends wear stuff _____ is a little too weird.
6. I usually buy clothes _____ are on sale.
7. I'm someone _____ likes reading fashion magazines.
8. I buy shoes _____ go with lots of different clothing.

B Pair work Make the sentences in Part A true for you. Tell your partner.

A: *I prefer salesclerks who don't say anything. I know what looks good on me.*
B: *Not me. I need all the help I can get!*

4 Speaking Thoughts on fashion

A Complete the sentences with your own ideas.

1. I really don't like clothes that are _____ .
2. _____ is a word which describes my personal style.
3. When shopping, I like friends who _____ .
4. _____ is a person who always looks fashionable.
5. I think _____ is a color that looks good on me.
6. A _____ is something that I never wear.
7. _____ is a designer who's very popular now.

B Group work Compare your ideas. Ask and answer questions for more information.

A: *I really don't like clothes that are expensive.*
B: *Really? I only like expensive clothes!*
C: *I like clothes that are comfortable.*

5 Keep talking!

Go to page 129 for more practice.

I can express opinions about style and fashion. ☑

D Views on fashion

1 Reading ◄))

A What's in style these days? Do you like the current fashions for men and women?

B Read the article. What is the survey about? Who took it, and where are they from?

FAVORITE FASHIONS

Image is important to many people, but what do men and women really think of each other's fashion choices? What do people actually think looks good on the opposite sex? An equal number of male and female university students in southern California recently answered some questions about fashion. Here are the results.

WHAT THE **GIRLS** SAID

What's the best color on a guy?
- **50%** Black
- **25%** White
- **25%** Whatever matches his eyes

What footwear looks the best on a guy?
- **60%** Flip-flops
- **25%** Dress shoes
- **15%** Skater shoes

What should a guy wear on a first date?
- **80%** Jeans, a nice shirt, and a jacket
- **15%** Shorts, a T-shirt, and flip-flops
- **5%** A shirt, a tie, and nice pants

WHAT THE **GUYS** SAID

What's the best color on a girl?
- **40%** Red
- **35%** White
- **25%** Black

What footwear looks the best on a girl?
- **45%** High heels
- **30%** High-top sneakers
- **25%** Flip-flops

What should a girl wear on a first date?
- **60%** Jeans and a classy top
- **25%** A black dress
- **15%** A short shirt and skirt

Source: Adapted from San Diego State University's student newspaper, *The Daily Aztec.*

C Read the article again. Are the sentences true or false? Write T (true) or F (false).

1. Fifty percent of the girls think a bright color looks best on a guy. _____
2. Girls like nice dress shoes on guys more than skater shoes. _____
3. Most girls think a guy should wear flip-flops on a first date. _____
4. Guys think white is the best color on a girl. _____
5. Guys like sneakers more than flip-flops on girls. _____
6. Most guys think girls should wear a black dress on a first date. _____

D **Pair work** Do you agree with the survey results? Why or why not? Discuss your ideas.

2 Listening An interview with Eduardo

A 🔊 Listen to an interview with Eduardo, a fashion designer. Number the questions from 1 to 5 in the order you hear them.

☐ Are high heels old-fashioned? ____

☐ Should belts and shoes be the same color? ____

☐ Does black go with everything? ____

☐ Is it OK for men to wear earrings? ____

☐ Can guys wear pink? ____

B 🔊 Listen again. How does Eduardo answer each question? Write Y (yes) or N (no).

C Do you agree with Eduardo's opinions? Why or why not?

3 Writing and speaking Class survey

A Group work Create a survey with four questions about fashion and style. Use the topics below or your own ideas.

cool places to shop	popular colors
current clothing styles	the latest gadgets
current hairstyles	trendy accessories
popular brands	unpopular colors

Fashion Survey
1. *What color is popular right now?*
2. *What's the most popular brand of jeans?*
3. *Where is a cool place to buy jewelry?*
4. *What gadget does everyone want now?*

B Class activity Ask and answer the questions in your surveys. Take notes.

C Group work Share and summarize the results.

Our Class Survey Results

Most people think blue is popular right now. Red was second and green was third. Only a few people think black, orange, or purple are popular. Only one person thinks yellow is popular.

The most popular brand of jeans is Sacco. A lot of people have these. Next was a brand called Durango. These were the only two brands that people mentioned.

Over half of the people in class think Glitter is a cool place to buy jewelry. Some people think the best place to buy jewelry is from people who sell it on the street. Two people . . .

D Class activity Share your most interesting results. Do you agree with the answers you heard? Give your own opinions.

I can ask and talk about current fashions. ☑

Wrap-up

1 Quick pair review

Lesson A Do you remember? Cross out the word that doesn't belong. Then write the category. You have two minutes.

1. _____	high heels	sandals	glasses
2. _____	a bracelet	contact lenses	earrings
3. _____	dyed hair	a uniform	a ponytail
4. _____	a uniform	high heels	a leather jacket
5. _____	glasses	contact lenses	earrings

Lesson B Brainstorm! Make a list of three ways to ask where something is and three ways to ask for an alternative. You have two minutes.

Lesson C Test your partner! Say each pair of sentences. Can your partner make them into one sentence with *which* or *who?* You have two minutes.

Student A

1. I'm a trendy person. I don't like old-fashioned clothes.
2. I usually wear glasses. They aren't glamorous.
3. Julie shops for stuff. It is affordable.

Student B

1. I usually wear hats. They are weird.
2. I know someone. She likes flashy bracelets.
3. Kyle is a guy. He wears tacky clothes.

A: *I'm a trendy person. I don't like old-fashioned clothes.*
B: *I'm a trendy person who doesn't like old-fashioned clothes.*

Lesson D Find out! What are two colors that both you and your partner think are good for girls to wear? What are two colors you both think are good for guys to wear? You have two minutes.

A: *I think pink is a good color for girls to wear. Do you?*
B: *No, but I think purple is a good color. Do you?*
A: *Yes.*

2 In the real world

What clothes used to be trendy? Go online and find examples of trendy clothes from one decade in the past. Then write about them.

1950s	1960s	1970s	1980s	1990s

Trends in the 1980s
Leg warmers used to be trendy in the 1980s. Tight jeans used to be popular, too. Women used to . . .

Interesting lives

Warm-up

A Describe the pictures. What are the people doing?

B Check (✓) the two most interesting activities. Have you ever done them?
If not, would you like to try them?

A *Have you ever been on TV?*

1 Vocabulary Experiences

A ◀)) Complete the phrases with the correct words. Then listen and check your answers.

an award	a famous person	on TV	to a new city
a bone	✓in a play	seasick	your phone

1. act *in a play*
2. be _____
3. break _____
4. get _____

5. lose _____
6. meet _____
7. move _____
8. win _____

B Pair work Which experiences in Part A are good to have? Which are not good to have? Discuss your ideas.

"It's good to win an award. It's not good to get seasick."

2 Language in context A local hero

A ◀)) Read Brian's online chat with some friends. Why is Brian excited?

○ ○ ○

Brian: You'll never believe what happened! I'm going to be on the TV news tonight! My first time!

Jill: You're kidding! Why?

Brian: It's a surprise. You have to watch. Have you ever been on TV?

Jill: No, I haven't. One of my friends is an actress, though, and I've seen her on TV a couple of times.

Hideo: I've never been on TV, but my sister Kumiko has been on TV lots of times. She's a TV reporter!

B What about you? Would you like to be on TV? Why or why not?

3 Grammar ◀)) **Present perfect**

Use the present perfect to describe events or experiences that happened at an unspecified time in the past. Use have / has *and the past participle of the verb.*

Have you ever **seen** a friend on TV?   **Has** your sister ever **been** on TV?

    Yes, I **have**.   Yes, she **has**.

    No, I **haven't**.   No, she **hasn't**.

Use frequency expressions with the present perfect to give more information.

I've **never** been on TV.   My sister has been on TV **lots of times**.

A Complete the conversations with the present perfect forms of the verbs. Then practice with a partner.

1. **A:** _____ you ever _____ (be) to another country?

   B: Yes, I _____ . I _____ (be) to Canada.

2. **A:** _____ you ever _____ (eat) sushi?

   B: Yes, I _____ . I _____ (have) it many times.

3. **A:** _____ you ever _____ (lose) your wallet?

   B: No, I _____ . Luckily, I _____ never _____ (lose) it.

4. **A:** _____ your best friend ever _____ (call) you in the middle of the night?

   B: No, she _____ . But I _____ (do) that to her once or twice!

B **Pair work** Ask and answer the questions in Part A. Answer with your own information.

◀)) **Regular past participles**

act	➤	act**ed**
chat	➤	chat**ted**
try	➤	tr**ied**

Irregular past participles

be	➤	**been**
break	➤	**broken**
do	➤	**done**
eat	➤	**eaten**
go	➤	**gone**
have	➤	**had**
lose	➤	**lost**
meet	➤	**met**
see	➤	**seen**
win	➤	**won**

Turn to page 151 for a list of more past participles.

4 Speaking Yes, I have!

A Complete the questions with your own ideas. Then check (✓) the things you've done, and write how often you've done them.

Have you ever . . . ?	Me	Name: _____	Name: _____
eaten _____	☐	☐	☐
been _____	☐	☐	☐
seen _____	☐	☐	☐
had _____	☐	☐	☐
won _____	☐	☐	☐
met _____	☐	☐	☐

B **Group work** Interview two classmates. Complete the chart with their answers. Who has had similar experiences?

5 Keep talking!

Go to page 130 for more practice.

I can ask and talk about life experiences. ☑

1 Interactions — Checking and clarifying meaning

A How often do you eat out? Do you ever cook at home? Do you ever order takeout?

B Listen to the conversation. How often does Sam eat out? Then practice the conversation.

Elena: I'm getting hungry.
Sam: Me, too.
Elena: Hey, Sam, there's a great Mexican restaurant near the school. Have you ever tried it?
Sam: No, I haven't. Actually, I don't eat in restaurants.
Elena: Really? Are you saying you never go to restaurants?
Sam: Well, no, not *never*. I mean I just don't eat out very often.
Elena: Why not?
Sam: I'm allergic to certain foods, like peanuts. If I eat them, my skin gets red and itchy.
Elena: That sounds awful!
Sam: It is!

C Read the expressions below. Complete each box with a similar expression from the conversation. Then listen and check your answers.

Checking meaning
_____
Do you mean . . . ?
Does that mean . . . ?

Clarifying meaning
_____
What I mean is, . . .
What I'm saying is, . . .

D Number the sentences in the conversation from 1 to 7. Then practice with a partner.

_____ A: What? Do you mean you never eat pizza?

_____ A: I see. So, when can I come over for homemade pizza?

_1_ A: I feel a little hungry.

_____ A: Have you ever been to Pizza Palace? We can go there.

_____ B: So do I.

_____ B: No, not *never*. What I mean is, I usually make it myself.

_____ B: Actually, I never go to fast-food places.

2 Pronunciation Contrastive stress in responses

A 🔊 Listen and repeat. Notice how the stressed words emphasize contrast.

Are you saying you never go to restaurants?

Well, not **never**. I mean I just don't eat out **very often**.

B Pair work Practice the conversation in Exercise 1D again. Stress words to emphasize contrast.

3 Listening Why not?

A 🔊 Listen to four conversations about habits and preferences. Correct the false information.

        never
1. Danielle ~~often~~ goes to hair salons.
2. Todd loves going to the beach.
3. Jessica always walks to school.
4. Mitch never rents DVDs.

B 🔊 Listen again. How do the people explain their habits and preferences? Check (✓) the correct answers.

1. Danielle's explanation:
   ☐ She finds it too expensive.
   ☐ Her sister cuts her hair.
   ☐ She cuts her own hair.

2. Todd's explanation:
   ☐ It's not easy to get there.
   ☐ He doesn't know how to swim.
   ☐ He doesn't like to be in the sun.

3. Jessica's explanation:
   ☐ The school is only five minutes away.
   ☐ She doesn't have a driver's license.
   ☐ She prefers to walk for the exercise.

4. Mitch's explanation:
   ☐ The movie theater is too far away.
   ☐ He thinks tickets are too expensive.
   ☐ He prefers to watch DVDs at home.

4 Speaking Unusual habits

A Write four statements about any unusual or interesting habits and behaviors you have. Use the questions to help you, or think of your own ideas.

- Is there a food you eat all the time?
- Is there a place you never go?
- Is there someone you talk to every day?
- Is there something you never do?
- Is there an expression you say all the time?

1. _____   3. _____
2. _____   4. _____

B Pair work Tell your partner about each habit or behavior. Your partner checks the meaning, and you clarify it. Take turns.

A: *I eat chocolate all the time.*
B: *Does that mean you eat it every day?*
A: *Well, no, not every day. I mean I have chocolate several times a week.*

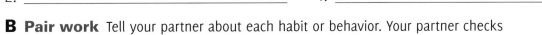

I can check and clarify meaning. ☑

37

C | *Life experiences*

1 Vocabulary Fun things to do

A 🔊 Match the phrases and the pictures. Then listen and check your answers.

a. climb a mountain	c. go camping	e. go whale-watching	g. try an exotic food
b. eat in a fancy restaurant	d. go to a spa	f. ride a roller coaster	h. try an extreme sport

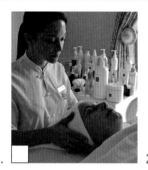 1. ☐
 2. ☐
 3. ☐
 4. ☐

 5. ☐
 6. ☐
 7. ☐
 8. ☐

B Pair work Have you ever done the fun things in Part A? Tell your partner.

2 Conversation A fancy restaurant

A 🔊 Listen to the conversation. Do you think Alice will order frog legs?

Alice: Wow! This place is nice!
Emma: Have you ever eaten in a fancy restaurant before?
Alice: Yes, I have. I've eaten in a few expensive restaurants, but this place is amazing.
Emma: You can try a lot of exotic food here, and all of their dishes are excellent. Oh, look. Tonight's special is frog legs.
Alice: Frog legs? Umm, I don't know. . . .
Emma: Have you ever tried them?
Alice: No, I haven't. But my brother tried them once a few years ago.
Emma: Did he like them?
Alice: I don't think so. He got sick later that night.

B 🔊 Listen to the rest of the conversation. What do Alice and Emma order?

3 Grammar ◄)) Present perfect vs. simple past

Use the present perfect to describe events or experiences at an unspecified time in the past.

Have you ever **eaten** in a fancy restaurant?

Yes, I **have**. I**'ve eaten** in a few expensive restaurants.

Use the simple past to describe events or experiences that happened at a specific time in the past.

Have you ever tried frog legs?

No, I haven't. But my brother **tried** them once **a few years ago**.

Did he **like** them?

I don't think so. He **got** sick later **that night**.

A Complete the conversations with the present perfect or simple past forms of the verbs. Then practice with a partner.

1. **A:** _____ you ever _____ (see) a whale?

   B: No, I _____ . But I _____ always _____ (want) to.

2. **A:** _____ you _____ (do) anything fun last weekend?

   B: Yes, I _____ . I _____ (go) camping with my sister.

3. **A:** _____ you ever _____ (eat) in a fancy restaurant?

   B: Yes, I _____ . I _____ (go) to Lucia's last year.

4. **A:** What extreme sports _____ you _____ (try)?

   B: I _____ (not / try) any. But my sister _____ (go) skydiving once!

5. **A:** What _____ you _____ (do) on your last vacation?

   B: My friend and I _____ (go) to a spa.

B **Pair work** Ask and answer the questions in Part A. Answer with your own information.

4 Speaking Is that true?

A Write two true sentences and one false sentence about interesting life experiences you've had.

1. _____

2. _____

3. _____

B **Group work** Share your sentences. Your group asks you questions and guesses the false sentence. Take turns.

A: *I've been to a wrestling match.*

B: *Really? Who did you go with?*

5 Keep talking!

Go to page 131 for more practice.

I can *describe details of my experiences.* ☑

D What a life!

1 Reading 🔊

A What do you think an astronaut's life is like? What do people need to do or know to become astronauts?

B Read the interview. According to Dr. Pettit, what's the most exciting thing he's experienced?

THE LIFE OF AN ASTRONAUT

Dr. Donald Pettit is a NASA astronaut.

Interviewer: I'm sure people ask you this question all of the time, Dr. Pettit, but I have to ask it: Have you ever been to space?

Dr. Pettit: Yes, I have. I was a crew member of *Expedition 6*, and I spent five and a half months at the International Space Station. We call it the ISS.

Interviewer: How many times have you gone up on the space shuttle?

Dr. Pettit: I've ridden the space shuttle to the ISS twice.

Interviewer: And what was the best part about being in space?

Dr. Pettit: Being able to float. It was the worst part, too.

Interviewer: Have you visited any other interesting places while working for NASA?

Dr. Pettit: Well, I lived in Russia for about two years while I was training to fly to the ISS. I've also been to Antarctica.

Interviewer: Not many people can say that! I understand that you like to work with tools. Have you ever invented anything?

Dr. Pettit: Yes. During my second trip into space, I made a special coffee cup so we could drink in space, much like we do here on earth. I just couldn't get used to drinking coffee out of a small bag through a straw!

Interviewer: I don't think I could get used to that, either. But why did you have to drink coffee that way before?

Dr. Pettit: Without the bag or my special cup, the coffee floats in space, too.

Interviewer: Of course! Well, you've accomplished so much, Dr. Pettit. Considering all of it, what's the most exciting thing that you've experienced?

Dr. Pettit: Seeing the birth of my twin boys.

Interviewer: Wow, what a life! Thanks so much for sharing, Dr. Pettit.

C Read the interview again. What things has Dr. Pettit done? Check (✓) the correct answers.

- ☐ walked on the moon
- ☐ been to the ISS
- ☐ ridden the space shuttle
- ☐ traveled to Antarctica
- ☐ had twin daughters
- ☐ invented something

D Pair work Would you like to travel to space? Why or why not? What would be the most interesting thing about it? Discuss your ideas.

2 Listening A memorable life

A 🔊 Listen to Leo ask his grandmother about her life. Number the questions from 1 to 5 in the order that you hear them.

☐ When did you meet Grandpa? _____

☐ What's something interesting you've done? _____

☐ Where else have you lived? _____

☐ Where were you born? _____

☐ Have you been back? _____

B 🔊 Listen again. Write the grandmother's answers to the questions in Part A.

3 Writing and speaking Interesting people, places, or things

A Choose one of the topics. Answer the questions.

Topics	Questions
A close friend I've had	Who is your friend? How exactly did you meet? Is this person your friend now? Why or why not?
A special place I've been	Where is this place? What made this place so special? Have you ever been back? Why or why not?
An interesting thing I've done	What did you do? How did you feel after doing it? Would you like to do it again? Why or why not?

B Write a paragraph about your topic. Use the model and your answers in Part A to help you.

My Friend Lucas

I've had several good friends, but one that was very special to me was my friend Lucas. He moved into the house next door when I was eight. We became good friends. We walked to school together and always played together at his house. He had a great bike, and I used to ride it. He moved to another city after a year. I've tried to find him online, but haven't had any luck. I . . .

C Pair work Read your partner's paragraph. Write five questions to get more information.

D Pair work Ask and answer your questions.

"So, tell me, why did you become friends?"

I **can** ask and talk about a memorable experience. ☑

Wrap-up

1 Quick pair review

Lesson A **Find out!** What is one place both you and your partner have been? one food you both have tried? one movie you both have seen? You have two minutes.

A: *I've been to the art museum downtown. Have you?*
B: *No, I haven't. I've been to our university library. Have you?*
A: *Yes, I have.*

Lesson B **Do you remember?** What can you say to clarify meaning? Check (✓) the correct answers. You have one minute.

☐ What I mean is, . . .   ☐ I didn't use to . . .

☐ What time is . . . ?   ☐ I mean . . .

☐ What I'm saying is, . . .   ☐ I used to go . . .

Lesson C **Brainstorm!** Imagine you and your partner are going on vacation together. Make a list of eight fun things to do on your trip. You have two minutes.

Lesson D **Guess!** Describe a memorable experience you've had, but don't say where it was. Can your partner guess where you were? You have two minutes.

2 In the real world

What do you think would be a memorable vacation? Find information in English online or in a travel magazine about one place. Then write about it.

> ### A Vacation in Hawaii
>
> Hawaii is a good place for a vacation. I've always wanted to go whale-watching, and I read that you can see whales in the Pacific Ocean from December to early May. The best places to see them are Maui, Molokai, and Lanai.
>
> I've also read about Haleakala National Park in Hawaii. A lot of people climb Mount Haleakala. I've seen pictures of it. It looks really beautiful. The weather is usually . . .

Our world

Warm-up

Shanghai World Financial Center – China

Tikal's Temple 4 – Guatemala

Poseidon Underwater Hotel – Fiji

The Parthenon – Greece

Grand Canyon Skywalk – U.S.

Palm Island – the U.A.E.

A Look at the pictures. Rank the places you would like to visit from 1 (the most) to 6 (the least).

B Why do you want to visit your top three places?

1 Vocabulary Human-made wonders

A 🔊 Label the pictures with the correct words. Then listen and check your answers.

bridge	plaza	stadium	tower
canal	skyscraper	subway system	tunnel

1. _____

2. _____

3. _____

4. _____

5. _____

6. _____

7. _____

8. _____

B **Pair work** Can you name a famous example for each word? Tell your partner.

"The Panama Canal is very famous."

2 Language in context Two amazing views

A 🔊 Read the question posted on a website for visitors to New York City. Which view does the site recommend?

Which is better, the view from the top of the Empire State Building or Rockefeller Center?

Good question! The Empire State Building is older, taller, and more famous than Rockefeller Center, so it gets more visitors. But the lines to get to the top of Rockefeller Center aren't as long as the lines at the Empire State Building. Tickets are more expensive, but I think the view is better. You can see Central Park on one side and the Empire State Building on the other!

B What about you? Where can you go in your town or city for a great view? Have you ever been there?

3 Grammar 🔊 **Comparisons with adjectives and nouns**

Use the -er *ending or* more . . . than *with adjectives to make comparisons.*
The Empire State Building is **older, taller**, and **more famous than** Rockefeller Center.

You can also use not as . . . as *to make comparisons with adjectives.*
The lines at Rockefeller Center are**n't as long as** the lines at the Empire State Building.
Tickets to the Empire State Building are**n't as expensive as** tickets to Rockefeller Center.

Use more . . . than *to make comparisons with nouns.*
The Empire State Building gets **more visitors than** Rockefeller Center.
Rockefeller Center has **more observation space than** the Empire State Building.

A Read the information about the Lincoln and Holland tunnels. Make comparisons with the adjectives and nouns below. Then compare with a partner.

LINCOLN TUNNEL
Year opened: 1937
Cars each day: 120,000
Length: 2.4 kilometers
Width: 6.5 meters
Number of traffic lanes: 6
Cost to build: $75 million

HOLLAND TUNNEL
Year opened: 1927
Cars each day: 100,000
Length: 2.6 kilometers
Width: 6 meters
Number of traffic lanes: 4
Cost to build: $48 million

1. (old)   The Lincoln Tunnel *isn't as old as the Holland Tunnel* .
2. (cars)   The Lincoln Tunnel _____ .
3. (long)   The Holland Tunnel _____ .
4. (wide)   The Holland Tunnel _____ .
5. (lanes)   The Lincoln Tunnel _____ .
6. (expensive) The Lincoln Tunnel _____ .

B Pair work Which tunnel do you think is more crowded? Why? Discuss your ideas.

4 Speaking Comparisons

Pair work Complete the chart with two examples of each place. Then make comparisons with the adjectives and nouns in the chart.

Places	Example 1	Example 2	Comparisons
cities			people? / exciting?
stadiums			old? / big?
skyscrapers			tall? / modern?
universities			expensive? / students?

A: *I'm sure . . . has more people than . . .*
B: *That's right. But I think . . . is more exciting than . . .*

5 Keep talking!

Student A go to page 132 and
Student B go to page 134 for more practice.

I can compare human-made structures. ☑

45

B I don't believe it!

1 Interactions Interesting and unknown facts

A What are the oldest human-made structures in your country? How old are they?

B 🔊 Listen to the conversation. What question can't Rachel answer?
Then practice the conversation.

Rachel: This is pretty interesting. Look at this.
Keith: What's that?
Rachel: I'm looking at this website about the statues on Easter Island. It says they've found almost 900 statues.
Keith: No way!
Rachel: Yes. Most of the statues face inland. Only a few of them face the sea.
Keith: When did the Easter Islanders make them?
Rachel: Let's see. . . . About 500 to 750 years ago.
Keith: They look so heavy, don't they?
Rachel: Yes, they do.
Keith: How did they move them?
Rachel: I really don't know. But let's see if we can find out.

C 🔊 Read the expressions below. Complete each box with a similar expression from the conversation. Then listen and check your answers.

Expressing disbelief

_____
Seriously?
I don't believe it!

Saying you don't know

_____
I have no idea.
I don't have a clue.

D **Pair work** Continue the conversation in Part B with these questions and answers. Use the expressions in Part C.

How tall is the tallest statue?	more than 20 meters tall!
Why did they stop building them?	(say you don't know)
How far is Easter Island from Chile?	more than 3,200 kilometers!
Do you think you'll ever go there?	(say you don't know)

2 Pronunciation Intonation in tag questions

A 🔊 Listen and repeat. Notice the falling intonation in tag questions when the speaker expects the listener to agree or expects something to be true.

The statues look so heavy, don't they? ⤵   The island is beautiful, isn't it? ⤴

B Pair work Practice the tag questions. Pay attention to your intonation.

1. Easter Island is part of Chile, isn't it?
2. You read that online, didn't you?
3. She wasn't sure, was she?
4. You've never been there, have you?
5. We should go there, shouldn't we?
6. They'll probably go there, won't they?

3 Listening "Manhattan of the Desert"

A 🔊 Listen to two people talk about the city of Shibam, in Yemen. Number the questions from 1 to 5 in the order you hear them.

☐ Is it easy to get to? _____

☐ How many people live there? _____

☐ What's it famous for? _____

☐ How high are the tallest buildings? _____

☐ How old is the city? _____

B 🔊 Listen again. Answer the questions in Part A.

4 Speaking Did you know . . . ?

A Make a list of three interesting facts about human-made structures.

1. There used to be soccer games and bullfights in the Plaza Mayor in Madrid, Spain.

2. More people ride the Tokyo Metro in Japan each year than any other subway system in the world.

3. The TV screen in Cowboys Stadium in Dallas, Texas, is almost 50 meters long!

B Group work Share your interesting facts. Your group expresses disbelief and asks questions for more information. If you don't know the answers to their questions, say you don't know.

A: *Did you know that there used to be soccer games and bullfights in the Plaza Mayor in Madrid, Spain?*
B: *Bullfights? Seriously? Why is it famous?*
A: *I don't have a clue.*

C How many questions could you answer correctly about the structures on your list? Which classmate could answer the most questions?

I can express disbelief. ☑
I can say that I don't know something. ☑

47

C World geography

1 Vocabulary Geographical features

A 🔊 Match the descriptions and the pictures. Then listen and check your answers.

a. The largest **desert** in Asia is the Gobi Desert.
b. There are about 17,000 **island**s in Indonesia.
c. Siberia's Lake Baikal is the world's deepest **lake**.
d. The Indian **Ocean** covers 20% of the earth's surface.
e. **Rain forest**s cover almost 75% of Brunei.
f. China's Yangtze River is the longest **river** in Asia.
g. Langtang Valley is one of the prettiest **valley**s in Nepal.
h. The highest **waterfall** in India is Jog Falls.

1.
2.
3.
4.
5.
6.
7.
8.

B **Pair work** What's another example of each geographical feature? Tell your partner.

2 Conversation Welcome to Bali.

A 🔊 Listen to the conversation. When does Bali get a lot of rain?

Guide: Welcome to Bali, one of the most beautiful islands in the world.

Sam: It's definitely the most beautiful island I've ever visited. Is Bali the biggest island in Indonesia?

Guide: No. Actually, it's one of the smallest, but it has a lot of people. The island of Java has the most people.

Sam: Is that right? The weather seems pretty nice right now. Is this the best time of year to visit?

Guide: Oh, yes. It's the dry season. We get the most sunshine this time of year. The wettest time is from November to April.

Sam: Well, that's good. Um, what's that?

Guide: Oh. It looks like rain.

B 🔊 Listen to the rest of the conversation. Why is Sam visiting Bali?

3 Grammar 🔊 | Superlatives with adjectives and nouns

Use the -est ending or the most to express the superlative with adjectives.

The wettest time is from November to April.
Bali is **the most beautiful** island I've ever visited.
The dry season is **the best** time to visit.

Use the most to express the superlative with nouns.

Java has **the most people** of all the islands in Indonesia.
Bali gets **the most sunshine** in the dry season.

A Complete the conversation with the superlative forms of the adjectives.
Then practice with a partner.

The Atacama Desert, Chile

A: I'm thinking of visiting Chile next year.

B: Great! You should try to visit my hometown, Viña del Mar.
One of _____ (popular) beaches in the
country is there. It's north of Santiago.

A: OK. Should I try to go to the Atacama Desert?

B: Definitely. I think it's _____ (beautiful)
part of the country. It's one of _____ (dry)
places in the world, too.

A: Cool. And how about Patagonia?

B: Well, that's in the south. Remember, Chile is
_____ (long) country in the world. It takes
time to see it all.

A: When's _____ (good) time to visit?

B: Anytime is fine. But I think _____ (nice)
time is between November and May.

B Pair work Make true sentences about your country with the phrases below.

| the most cars | the most fun | the most rain | the most tourists |

4 Speaking Tell me about it.

A Group work Discuss your experiences in different geographical locations.

- What's the most beautiful island you've ever seen?
- What's the coldest lake, river, or ocean you've ever swum in?
- What's the highest mountain you've ever climbed?
- What's the prettiest geographical location you've ever taken a picture of?
- What's the most amazing place you've ever walked through?

B Share your information. Who has had the most interesting experience?

5 Keep talking!

Go to page 133 for more practice.

I can ask and talk about geographical features. ☑

D Natural wonders

1 Reading 🔊

A What do you think is the most amazing natural wonder in the world? Why?

B Read the article. What are the seven wonders, and where are they?

Seven Wonders of the Natural World

Here is a list of some of the most fascinating places in the world.

The Rio de Janeiro Harbor in Brazil is one of the biggest and most amazing harbors in the world. It has beautiful beaches and the famous Sugar Loaf Mountain.

Over five million people visit the Grand Canyon in the U.S. state of Arizona every year. The breathtaking landscape is 445 kilometers long, 24 kilometers wide, and more than a kilometer deep!

The Great Barrier Reef is not just one colorful coral reef. It's actually almost 3,000 of them! Many plants and gorgeous tropical fish live among these reefs off the coast of Australia.

Located in the Himalayas on the border of Nepal and Tibet, Mount Everest is the highest mountain in the world – and one of the most dangerous to climb. But that doesn't stop people from trying to get to the top of it every year!

Have you ever heard the crashing sound of millions of liters of water? The Zambezi River between Zambia and Zimbabwe falls 120 meters, making Victoria Falls one of the largest and loudest waterfalls on the planet.

Paricutín Volcano in Mexico is more than 300 meters high, but it used to be a flat cornfield. In 1943, people saw the earth steam and crack. It grew into a new volcano in just two years!

The Northern Lights are exactly what their name suggests: bright, flashing lights of amazing shapes and colors in the northern sky. The North Pole has the best view of them.

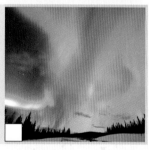

C Read the article again. Complete the sentences with the correct natural wonders.

1. _____ has beautiful beaches.
2. _____ is a very loud waterfall.
3. _____ is over a kilometer deep.
4. _____ formed in two years.
5. _____ change in shape and color.
6. _____ is off a country's coast.

D Pair work Rank the natural wonders from 1 (most amazing) to 7 (least amazing). Then compare answers.

2 **Listening** The Great Barrier Reef

A 🔊 Listen to a guide talk to two tourists at the Great Barrier Reef.
Which statements surprise the tourists? Check (✓) the correct answers.

☐ The Great Barrier Reef is made up of many smaller reefs.
☐ You can see the reef from space.
☐ You can see turtles near the reef.
☐ Global warming can make the coral appear white.

B 🔊 Listen again. Answer the questions.

1. How many kinds of coral are there? _____
2. How does the coral look on TV? _____
3. What's the weather like today? _____
4. What does the guide say to do? _____

3 **Writing** A natural wonder

A Think of a natural wonder in your country. Answer the questions.

* Where is it? _____
* What does it look like? _____
* What can you do there? _____
* When's a good time to go there? _____

B Write a paragraph about the natural wonder. Use the model and your answers in
Part A to help you.

A Wonderful Mountain
Mount Toubkal is the highest mountain in
Morocco, and one of the prettiest. The most
popular time to visit is the summer. Many
people climb the mountain, and you can hike
it in two days. To me, the most interesting
time to visit is the winter because you can
ski. This is surprising to many people. . . .

C Group work Share your paragraphs. Can anyone add more information?

4 **Speaking** Seven wonders of my country

A Pair work Make a list of the top seven natural or human-made wonders in your
country. Why are they wonderful? Take notes.

B Class activity Share your lists and reasons. Then vote on the top seven
wonders to create one list.

I can describe natural wonders in my country. ☑

Wrap-up

1 Quick pair review

Lesson A Brainstorm! Make a list of human-made wonders. How many do you know? You have one minute.

Lesson B Do you remember? Is the sentence expressing disbelief, or is it saying you don't know? Write D (disbelief) or DK (don't know). You have one minute.

1. I have no idea. _____
2. Seriously? _____
3. No way! _____
4. I don't believe it! _____
5. I don't have a clue. _____
6. I really don't know. _____

Lesson C Test your partner! Say three comparative adjectives. Can your partner use the superlative forms in a sentence? Take turns. You have three minutes.

A: *More famous.*
B: *The most famous. The most famous person I've ever met is George Clooney.*

Lesson D Guess! Describe a natural wonder in your country, but don't say its name. Can your partner guess what it is? You have two minutes.

2 In the real world

What are the seven wonders of the modern world? Go online or to a library, and find information in English about the seven wonders of the modern world. Choose one and write about it.

> ### A Wonder of the Modern World
> The Itaipu Dam is one of the seven wonders of the modern world. It's on the Paraná River between Brazil and Paraguay. Many people in South America depend on the dam for power and electricity. About 40,000 workers helped construct the dam, and it's one of the most expensive objects ever built. It's also huge. In fact, it's so big that . . .

Organizing your time

LESSON **A**	LESSON **B**	LESSON **C**	LESSON **D**
• Commitments • Present tenses used for future	• Offering to take a message • Leaving a message	• Favors • Requests; promises and offers with *will*	• Reading: "How to Manage Your Time" • Writing: Tips for success

Warm-up

A Look at the pictures. What's happening? Do you think the man organizes his time well?

B Do you think you organize your time well? Why or why not?

A *A busy week*

1 Vocabulary Commitments

A 🔊 Match the words in columns A and B. Then listen and check your answers.

A	B
1. a birthday	appointment
2. a blind	call
3. a business	date
4. a conference	interview
5. a doctor's	lesson
6. a job	meeting
7. soccer	party
8. a violin	practice

B Pair work When was the last time you had each commitment? Tell your partner.

2 Language in context Weekend plans

A 🔊 Read George's plans for the weekend. Number the pictures from 1 to 8.

My parents are arriving from out of town this weekend. I'm picking them up at the airport on Friday night. Their flight doesn't get in until midnight. They're staying at my place for a couple of weeks. On Saturday, I'm preparing breakfast for them. Then I have a doctor's appointment. In the afternoon, I'm taking them for a drive around town. In the evening, I'm starting a new part-time job. There's a new movie I want to see on Sunday. I'm going with a friend of mine from school. It starts at 9:00 p.m., so we're having dinner first.

B Which things in Part A do you think George will enjoy? Do you have any of the same plans?

3 Grammar ◀》 Present tenses used for future

Use the present continuous to describe plans or intentions.
My parents **are arriving** from out of town this weekend.
They**'re staying** at my place for the weekend.

Use the simple present to describe events that are on a schedule or a timetable.
I **have** an appointment in the morning.
The movie **starts** at 9:00 p.m.

A Complete the conversation with the present continuous or the simple present forms of the verbs. Then practice with a partner.

A: What _____ you _____ (do) tonight?
B: Oh, I _____ (take) my sister to the airport. She _____ (go) to Manila. Her flight _____ (leave) at 9:00.
A: _____ you _____ (do) anything tomorrow?
B: I _____ (have) soccer practice at 2:00.

B Pair work What are your plans after class? Tell your partner.

4 Listening A weekend away

A ◀》 Listen to Peter talk with his neighbor Nancy. Check (✓) the true sentences.

1. ☐ Nancy has a date this weekend. _____
2. ☐ Peter's train leaves Friday night at 8:30. _____
3. ☐ Peter's grandfather is turning 70. _____
4. ☐ Peter and Kevin are going to museums on Sunday. _____
5. ☐ Peter and Kevin arrive home on Sunday evening. _____
6. ☐ Peter has a job interview on Monday. _____

B ◀》 Listen again. Correct the false sentences.

5 Speaking What are you doing this weekend?

A Class activity Find classmates who are going to do each thing. Write their names and ask questions for more information.

Find someone who . . . this weekend.	Name	Extra information
is going out		
is planning to stay home		
has a lesson or an appointment		
plans to meet friends		
is spending time with relatives		

B Who has the most interesting plans? What are they?

6 Keep talking!

Go to page 135 for more practice.

I can ask and talk about weekend plans. ☑

B Can I take a message?

1 Interactions | Phone messages

A How many phone calls do you make in a week? Do you leave many messages?

B 🔊 Listen to the conversation. What message does Rex leave for Jake?
Then practice the conversation.

Ben: Hello?
Rex: Hi. Can I please speak to Jake?
Ben: Um, sorry. Jake's not here right now. I think he might be at the gym.
Can I take a message?
Rex: Uh, sure. This is Rex Hanson. I'm calling about our class trip. Please tell
him that we're leaving tomorrow at 8:00, not 9:00.
Ben: OK, got it. I'll give him the message.
Rex: Great. Thanks a lot. Bye.
Ben: Good-bye.

C 🔊 Read the expressions below. Complete each box with a similar expression from
the conversation. Then listen and check your answers.

Offering to take a message

_____
Do you want to leave a message?
Would you like to leave a message?

Leaving a message

_____
Can you tell . . . that . . . ?
Could you let . . . know that . . . ?

D Pair work Have conversations like the one in Part B. Use these ideas.

You're calling your friend Carrie at home, but she's at soccer practice.	You're calling your friend Gary at work, but he's in a meeting.
She needs to bring her laptop to class.	The birthday party starts at 7:00, not 8:00.

2 Listening Taking messages

A 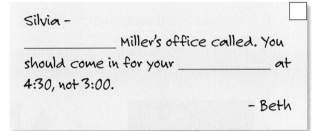 Listen to four people leave phone messages. Number the messages from 1 to 4.

Manhattan **Designs** ☐
TO: Mr. Philips
FROM: Julie Kim
TIME: 2:45
MESSAGE:
She needs the _____ for her office by _____ .

Silvia – ☐
_____ Miller's office called. You should come in for your _____ at 4:30, not 3:00.

– Beth

Paul, ☐
Your _____ Kurt called. Your parents' anniversary party is at his place, not your _____ .

MESSAGE ☐
To: Roberto
From: Hank
Message:
_____ is canceled _____ .

B Listen again. Complete the messages.

C Listen to the people return the calls. What happens to whom?
Write M (Mr. Philips), P (Paul), R (Roberto), or S (Silvia).

1. _____ gets a busy signal.   3. _____ leaves a voicemail.

2. _____ gets disconnected.   4. _____ calls the wrong number.

3 Speaking Role play

A Complete the chart with your own ideas.

	Who's the message for?	What's the message about?	What's the message?
1.	Rosario	soccer practice	She needs to come 15 minutes early.
2.		the meeting	It's on Thursday, not Tuesday. It's still at 4:00.
3.	Jennifer		It starts at 10:00 p.m. Bring dancing shoes.
4.		the job interview	
5.			

B Pair work Role-play the phone conversations. Then change roles.

Student A: Call the people in the chart. They can't talk, so leave messages for them.

Student B: Answer the phone. Explain why the people can't talk, and offer to take messages for them.

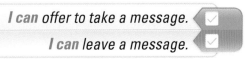

I can offer to take a message. ☑
I can leave a message. ☑

C Can you do me a favor?

1 Vocabulary Favors

A 🔊 Match the phrases and the pictures. Then listen and check your answers.

a. check my homework	c. get my mail	e. help me with my résumé	g. pick me up
b. feed my cat	d. give me a ride	f. lend me some money	h. water my plants

 1. ☐

 2. ☐

 3. ☐

 4. ☐

 5. ☐

 6. ☐

 7. ☐

 8. ☐

B Pair work Who might you ask to do each thing in Part A? Discuss your ideas.

a child	a classmate	a friend	a neighbor	a parent	a teacher

2 Conversation Is that all?

A 🔊 Listen to the conversation. What things does Kate ask Ruth to do for her?

Ruth: Oh, hi, Kate. What's up?

Kate: Hi, Ruth. Listen, I'm going away this weekend. Can you do me a favor?

Ruth: Sure. What do you need?

Kate: Can you feed my cat, please?

Ruth: No problem. I'll feed her. Is that all?

Kate: Well, could you please get my mail, too?

Ruth: Sure. I could do that for you. I'll put it on your kitchen table. Anything else?

Kate: If you don't mind, there's one more thing.

Ruth: What's that?

Kate: I'm getting back at 11:00 on Sunday night. Would you mind picking me up at the airport?

B 🔊 Listen to the rest of the conversation. Why can't Ruth pick Kate up?

3 Grammar 🔊 | Requests; promises and offers with *will*

Requests	Promises and offers
Can you **feed** my cat, please?	No problem. **I'll feed** her.
Could you please **get** my mail?	Sure. **I'll put** it on your kitchen table.
Would you **pick** me up at the airport?	All right. **I won't be** late. I promise.
Would you **mind picking** me up at the airport?	No, I don't mind. **I'll be** there.

A Match the requests and the responses. Then practice with a partner.

1. Can you lend me your car tonight? _____
2. Ms. Smith, would you check my homework, please? _____
3. Can you give me a ride to class? _____
4. Would you mind feeding my fish? _____
5. Could you water my plants this weekend? _____
6. Would you mind picking me up at the mall? _____

a. Sure. I'll look at it after I help Michael.
b. No problem. I'll do it on Saturday.
c. Not at all. What time?
d. I guess so. I'll give you the keys after I pick up Rachel from school.
e. Yeah, sure. I'll be at your house at 10:00.
f. No, I don't mind. I'll feed them after work.

B Pair work Ask and answer the questions in Part A. Answer with your own offer or promise.

4 Pronunciation Reduction of *could you* and *would you*

A 🔊 Listen and repeat. Notice how *could you* and *would you* are sometimes pronounced /kʊdʒə/ and /wʊdʒə/.

Could you please get my mail?   **Would you** pick me up at the airport?

B Pair work Practice requests with *could you, would you*, and the phrases from Exercise 1. Reduce *could you* and *would you*.

5 Speaking Unfavorable favors

A Think of three favors to ask your classmates. Use the ideas below or your own ideas. Be creative!

feed my pet snake	lend me some money
check my homework	lend me your cell phone
help me clean my room	make my lunch

B Class activity Find three different classmates to do the favors for you. If you decline a request, make an excuse. If you accept a request, make an offer or a promise.

6 Keep talking!

Go to page 136 for more practice.

I can make requests, promises, and offers. ☑

D Time management

1 Reading))

A Do you have a busy schedule? What's the busiest day of your week?

B Read the headings in the article. Which things do you do to manage your time?

HOW TO MANAGE YOUR TIME

These simple ideas can help you manage your time and work more effectively. Share these tips with your friends, family, or co-workers.

1. Write things down.
Don't try to remember every detail. This can cause information overload. Make a list so you don't forget what you have to do.

2. Put your list in order.
Put the most important things in your list at the top. This helps you spend time on the things that matter most.

3. Plan your week.
Spend some time at the beginning of each week to plan your schedule. All you need is 15 to 30 minutes each week.

4. Carry a notebook.
You never know when you'll have a great idea. Carry a small notebook with you so you can write down your thoughts.

5. Learn to say no.
Many people say yes when they should say no. Say no when you need to. Then you'll have time to spend on more important things.

6. Think before you act.
Don't always agree to do something right away. Think about it before you answer. You don't want to commit to too much.

7. Continuously improve yourself.
Make time to learn new things and develop your natural talents. Try to improve your knowledge and skills.

8. Identify bad habits.
Make a list of bad habits that are wasting your time and slowing your success. Then work on them one at a time.

9. Don't do other people's work.
Are you in the habit of doing other people's work? This can take up a lot of time. Think about your own goals. Leave some things for other people to do.

10. Don't try to be perfect.
Some things don't need your best effort. Learn the difference between more important and less important jobs.

C Read the article and the statements below. What's the best time-management tip for each person to follow? Write the number of the tip.

1. "I often make decisions quickly. Then, of course, I'm sorry I made them." _____

2. "I'm always forgetting things. My memory is terrible. It's embarrassing!" _____

3. "I spend too much time on tasks that don't matter." _____

4. "I find excuses to avoid doing my own work. I shouldn't do that, but I do." _____

5. "I always agree to things when I know I shouldn't. I feel like I need to say yes!" _____

6. "I want everything I do to be the best it can be." _____

D Pair work Which tips do you think are very useful? not very useful? Why? Discuss your ideas.

2 Writing Tips for success

A Group work Choose one of the topics below or your own idea. What tips for success can you think of? Discuss your ideas and make a list of your tips.

how to find more time for family	how to remember important things
how to make and keep friends	how to study better

B Group work Create a poster with the most useful tips. Write a short paragraph for each tip.

C Class activity Present your tips for success. Ask and answer questions for more information.

HOW TO DEVELOP BETTER STUDY HABITS

1. Take regular breaks.
It's important to take breaks. Get up and stretch, go for a walk, or call a friend for a chat. You'll feel ready for more!

2. Listen to music.
Listen to relaxing music. This helps you . . .

3 Speaking Time management interview

A Pair work Interview your partner. Check (✓) his or her answers.

Are you overdoing things?

Do you . . . ?	Often	Sometimes	Never
get nervous when you have to wait	☐	☐	☐
feel like you do things too quickly	☐	☐	☐
often do two or more things at once	☐	☐	☐
feel bad when you're not working or studying	☐	☐	☐
feel like things don't move fast enough for you	☐	☐	☐
forget important events, like birthdays	☐	☐	☐
get angry in situations you can't control	☐	☐	☐
get bored easily when you're not working or studying	☐	☐	☐
get angry when you make small mistakes	☐	☐	☐
make big decisions before you get all the facts	☐	☐	☐

B Pair work Score your partner's answers. Add 2 for *often*, 1 for *sometimes*, and 0 for *never*. Tell your partner the results.

13–20 You're overdoing it.
You probably already know you're too busy. Take a deep breath and slow down.

7–12 You're overdoing it a little.
You're doing well, but try not to do too much. Make sure you make time for yourself.

0–6 You're not overdoing it.
Congratulations! You are managing your time well. Keep it up!

C Pair work Are you overdoing it? If so, what time-management tips can help? Discuss your ideas.

I can discuss ways to manage time effectively.

Wrap-up

1 Quick pair review

Lesson A Find out! What are two commitments both you and your partner have next month? You have two minutes.

A: *I'm going to a conference for work next month. Are you?*
B: *No, I'm not, but I have a dentist's appointment next month. Do you?*
A: *. . .*

Lesson B Brainstorm! Make a list of three ways to offer to take a message and three ways to leave one. You have two minutes.

Lesson C Do you remember? Match the requests and the responses. You have two minutes.

1. Could you water my plants for me? _____
2. Would you mind giving me a ride to work? _____
3. Can you feed my dog, please? _____
4. Could you please call me back at 4:00? _____
5. Can you meet me in the library tomorrow? _____

a. OK. I'll call your cell phone.
b. Sure. I'll water them.
c. Yes. I'll bring my books so we can study.
d. Yeah, I'll do that. What does he eat?
e. No problem. I'll pick you up at 8:00.

Lesson D Give your opinion! What three tips can you give someone who is always late for class? Decide together. You have two minutes.

2 In the real world

What are some tips for success? Go online and find tips in English about one of these topics or your own idea. Then write about them.

how to get rich	how to make a good first impression
how to improve your pronunciation	how to write a good résumé

How to Save Money
It's important to save money every month. One way to save money is to turn off the lights when you aren't using them, because electricity is expensive. Another way to save money is to cook at home more often. Food can be very expensive, especially if you eat out a lot. You should look for coupons in newspapers. Also, . . .

Finding out more

A Read the chart. Then add two more questions.

Find someone who . . .	Name	Extra information
is saving money for something special		
is in a good mood today		
has one brother and one sister		
is reading an interesting book		
wants to get a pet		
is taking a difficult class		
works on weekends		
thinks English is fun		
hates to talk on the phone		

B Class activity Find classmates who do or are doing each thing in Part A. Write their names. Ask questions for more information.

A: *Are you saving money for something special?*
B: *Yes, I am.*
A: *Oh, really? What do you want to buy?*

C Class activity Share the most interesting information.

Similar behaviors

A Write your answers to the questions in the chart.

Questions	Me	Name: _____
1. What do you do when you can't sleep at night?		
2. What do you do if you forget to do your homework?		
3. When you feel really happy about something, what do you do?		
4. What do you do if someone tells you something that isn't true?		
5. If a friend calls you and you don't want to talk, what do you do?		
6. What do you do when you are extremely angry at someone?		

B **Pair work** Interview your partner. Complete the chart with his or her answers.

A: *What do you do when you can't sleep at night?*
B: *I usually read a book. How about you?*
A: *When I can't sleep at night, I always listen to music.*

C **Pair work** Compare your information. Do any of your partner's answers surprise you? Do you and your partner have any similar behaviors?

What was happening?

A Look at this picture for two minutes. What was happening when it started to rain? Try to remember as many details as you can.

B Pair work Cover the picture. Ask the questions and answer with the information you remember.

1. Where was the couple sitting when the rain started? What were they doing?
2. What was the police officer holding? What was she wearing?
3. What was the name of the café? What was on the café table?
4. What was the waiter holding? Where was he standing?
5. What was the young boy holding? What was he watching on TV?
6. What was the taxi driver doing? What was the name of the cab company?

C Pair work Check your answers. How many answers did you remember correctly?

How does it end?

A **Pair work** Imagine you are the people in one of the sets of pictures below.
Tell a story that explains what happened. Choose your own ending to the story.

Story 1

Story 2

B **Group work** Tell your story to another pair. Can they think of another ending
to your story? Which ending do you like better?

*"This really happened to us. We were driving down the road in our car. The weather
was very nice, and we were enjoying the ride. We were going to our friend's house.
We had a map, but suddenly . . ."*

C **Class activity** Share your stories. Vote on the best one.

Then and now

Student A

A **Pair work** You and your partner have pictures of Chuck. You have an old picture of what he used to look like, and your partner has a new picture of what he looks like now. Describe Chuck to find the differences between then and now.

Chuck – then

A: *Chuck used to have long black hair.*
B: *He doesn't have long hair now.*
A: *So that's different. He used to . . .*

B **Pair work** You and your partner have pictures of Amy. You have a new picture of what she looks like now, and your partner has an old picture of what she used to look like. Describe Amy to find the differences between then and now.

Amy – now

Then and now

Student B

A Pair work You and your partner have pictures of Chuck. You have a new picture of what he looks like now, and your partner has an old picture of what he used to look like. Describe Chuck to find the differences between then and now.

Chuck – now

A: *Chuck used to have long black hair.*
B: *He doesn't have long hair now.*
A: *So that's different. He used to . . .*

B Pair work You and your partner have pictures of Amy. You have an old picture of what she used to look like, and your partner has a new picture of what she looks like now. Describe Amy to find the differences between then and now.

Amy – then

What's hot?

A Write your own example of each thing in the chart.

Give an example of . . .	Me	Name: _____
something which looks tacky on young people		
an area of town that's extremely trendy		
a store that's very popular with young people		
a male celebrity who's really fashionable		
a female celebrity who's very glamorous		
a fashion trend that was very weird		
a fashion that you really like		
someone that has influenced fashion		

B Pair work Interview your partner. Complete the chart with his or her answers.

A: *What is something which you think looks tacky on young people?*
B: *Well, I don't like those big sunglasses that some young girls wear. I think they're tacky.*

C Class activity Compare your information. Do you agree with everyone's opinion? Why or why not?

A: *I think . . . is a celebrity who's very glamorous.*
B: *Really? I think her clothes are kind of weird.*
C: *I like most of the clothes that she wears. I think she has a lot of style.*

I've never . . .

A Write examples of things you've never done.

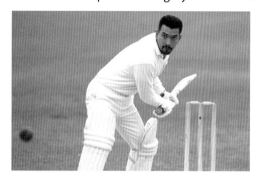

a sport I've never played:

_____

a TV show I've never watched:

_____

a food I've never eaten:

_____

a famous movie I've never seen:

_____

a restaurant I've never been to:

_____

a place I've never visited:

_____

B **Group work** Tell your group about the things you've never done. Ask and answer questions for more information.

> **A:** _I've never played cricket._
> **B:** _Yeah, that's not popular here at all._
> **C:** _I've never played basketball._
> **D:** _You're kidding! Never? Not even in school?_

C **Class activity** Share your information. Which answers surprised you the most?

No kidding!

A Add two more questions about experiences to the chart.

Have you ever . . . ?	Name	Extra information
seen a solar eclipse		
watched three movies in one day		
gone swimming in the rain		
gotten a postcard from overseas		
cooked a vegetarian dinner		
seen a shooting star		
had a really bad haircut		
forgotten to pay an important bill		
eaten in a French restaurant		
lost something very special to you		

a solar eclipse

a shooting star

B Class activity Find classmates who have done each thing. Write their names and ask questions for more information.

    A: *Have you ever seen an eclipse?*
    B: *Yes, I have. I saw a solar eclipse once.*
    A: *No kidding! When did you see it?*

C Share the most interesting information.

Impressive places

Student A

A You and your partner have information about impressive places. Do you know the answers to the questions on the left? Circle your guesses.

1. Which is taller?
   a. Eiffel Tower (Paris, France)
   b. CN Tower (Toronto, Canada)

a. ☐ 300.5 meters tall   b. ☐ _____ meters tall

2. Which is longer?
   a. Golden Gate Bridge (San Francisco, the U.S.A.)
   b. Harbor Bridge (Sydney, Australia)

a. ☐ _____ meters long   b. ☐ 1,149 meters long

3. Which is bigger?
   a. Red Square (Moscow, Russia)
   b. Tiananmen Square (Beijing, China)

 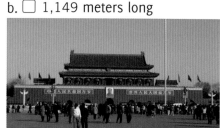

a. ☐ 23,100 square meters   b. ☐ _____ square meters

4. Which has more riders?
   a. São Paulo subway system (Brazil)
   b. London subway system (the U.K.)

a. ☐ _____ riders a day   b. ☐ 4,250,000 riders a day

B Pair work Ask and answer questions to fill in the missing information. Then check (✓) the correct answers in Part A.

How tall is . . . ?
How long is . . . ?
How big is . . . ?
How many riders does . . . have?

Saying large numbers
100.2   "one hundred point two"
3,456   "three thousand four hundred (and) fifty-six"
78,900   "seventy-eight thousand nine hundred"
120,000   "one hundred (and) twenty thousand"
3,450,000   "three million four hundred (and) fifty thousand"

C Class activity How many of your guesses were correct? Can you make more comparisons?

Planning a visit

A **Pair work** Imagine that a friend from another country is planning to visit you and asks you the questions in the email below. Discuss your responses.

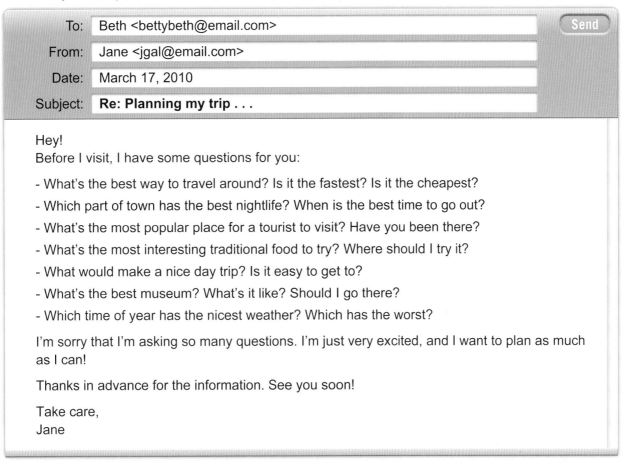

To: Beth <bettybeth@email.com>   **Send**
From: Jane <jgal@email.com>
Date: March 17, 2010
Subject: **Re: Planning my trip . . .**

Hey!
Before I visit, I have some questions for you:

- What's the best way to travel around? Is it the fastest? Is it the cheapest?
- Which part of town has the best nightlife? When is the best time to go out?
- What's the most popular place for a tourist to visit? Have you been there?
- What's the most interesting traditional food to try? Where should I try it?
- What would make a nice day trip? Is it easy to get to?
- What's the best museum? What's it like? Should I go there?
- Which time of year has the nicest weather? Which has the worst?

I'm sorry that I'm asking so many questions. I'm just very excited, and I want to plan as much as I can!

Thanks in advance for the information. See you soon!

Take care,
Jane

A: *The best way to travel around is by subway.*
B: *I think it's better to go by bus. It's faster than the subway.*

B **Group work** Share your ideas with another pair. Do you have similar answers?

Impressive places

Student B

A You and your partner have information about impressive places. Do you know the answers to the questions on the left? Circle your guesses.

1. Which is taller?
   a. Eiffel Tower
      (Paris, France)
   b. CN Tower
      (Toronto, Canada)

a. ☐ _____ meters tall   b. ☐ 553.3 meters tall

2. Which is longer?
   a. Golden Gate Bridge
      (San Francisco, the
      U.S.A.)
   b. Harbor Bridge
      (Sydney, Australia)

a. ☐ 2,737 meters long   b. ☐ _____ meters long

3. Which is bigger?
   a. Red Square
      (Moscow, Russia)
   b. Tiananmen Square
      (Beijing, China)

a. ☐ _____ square meters   b. ☐ 440,000 square meters

4. Which has more riders?
   a. São Paulo subway
      system
      (Brazil)
   b. London subway system
      (the U.K.)

a. ☐ 3,500,000 riders a day   b. ☐ _____ riders a day

B Pair work Ask and answer questions to fill in the missing information. Then check (✓) the correct answers in Part A.

How tall is . . . ?
How long is . . . ?
How big is . . . ?
How many riders does . . . have?

Saying large numbers

100.2	"one hundred point two"
3,456	"three thousand four hundred (and) fifty-six"
78,900	"seventy-eight thousand nine hundred"
120,000	"one hundred (and) twenty thousand"
3,450,000	"three million four hundred (and) fifty thousand"

C Class activity How many of your guesses were correct? Can you make more comparisons?

The next two weeks

A Complete the calendars for next week and the week after it with the correct dates and any plans you have.

Next week:

Monday	Tuesday	Wednesday	Thursday	Friday	Saturday	Sunday

The week after next:

Monday	Tuesday	Wednesday	Thursday	Friday	Saturday	Sunday

B Pair work Ask and answer questions about your plans. Find a time to do something together.

A: *What are you doing next Thursday afternoon?*
B: *Oh, I have my karate lesson then. What are you doing the day after that?*
A: *Nothing. Do you want to get together?*

C Group work Tell another pair about the plans you made in Part B. Invite them to join you. Are they free?

A: *Barry and I are getting together on Friday.*
B: *We're meeting at Mr. Freeze for some ice cream. Do you want to join us?*
C: *I'm sorry, but I can't. I have a job interview on Friday.*
D: *I'm not free, either. I have to go grocery shopping.*

A helping hand

A Pair work Imagine you're the people in the pictures. Role-play the situations.

Student A: Ask Student B for a favor.
Student B: Agree to Student A's request. Offer to help, and continue the conversation.

A: *Could you do me a favor? Could you please take my picture?*
B: *No problem. I'll take it for you.*

B Pair work Change roles. Role-play the new situations.

C Pair work Ask each other for two more favors.

Irregular verbs

Base form	Simple past	Past participle
be	was, were	been
become	became	become
break	broke	broken
build	built	built
buy	bought	bought
choose	chose	chosen
come	came	come
do	did	done
draw	drew	drawn
drink	drank	drunk
drive	drove	driven
eat	ate	eaten
fall	fell	fallen
feel	felt	felt
fly	flew	flown
forget	forgot	forgotten
get	got	gotten
give	gave	given
go	went	gone
hang	hung	hung
have	had	had
hear	heard	heard
hold	held	held
know	knew	known
leave	left	left

Base form	Simple past	Past participle
lose	lost	lost
make	made	made
meet	met	met
pay	paid	paid
put	put	put
read	read	read
ride	rode	ridden
run	ran	run
say	said	said
see	saw	seen
sell	sold	sold
send	sent	sent
sing	sang	sung
sit	sat	sat
sleep	slept	slept
speak	spoke	spoken
spend	spent	spent
stand	stood	stood
swim	swam	swum
take	took	taken
teach	taught	taught
think	thought	thought
wear	wore	worn
win	won	won
write	wrote	written

Adjective and adverb formations

Adjectives	Adverbs	Adjectives	Adverbs
agreeable	agreeably	immature	immaturely
amazing	amazingly	impatient	impatiently
ambitious	ambitiously	inconsiderate	inconsiderately
angry	angrily	indecisive	indecisively
brave	bravely	interesting	interestingly
careful	carefully	late	late
confident	confidently	lucky	luckily
considerate	considerately	mature	maturely
creative	creatively	nervous	nervously
curious	curiously	optimistic	optimistically
decisive	decisively	patient	patiently
disagreeable	disagreeably	quick	quickly
dishonest	dishonestly	rare	rarely
early	early	reliable	reliably
easy	easily	sad	sadly
enthusiastic	enthusiastically	serious	seriously
extreme	extremely	similar	similarly
fair	fairly	strange	strangely
fashionable	fashionably	stubborn	stubbornly
fast	fast	sudden	suddenly
fortunate	fortunately	surprising	surprisingly
glamorous	glamorously	unfair	unfairly
good	well	unfortunate	unfortunately
hard	hard	unreliable	unreliably
honest	honestly	wise	wisely

Credits

Four Corners

Jack C. Richards · David Bohlke

3A

Video Activity Sheets

CAMBRIDGE
UNIVERSITY PRESS

Credits

Photography credits

T-180, T-181 (bottom), T-182, T-183, T-184, T-185, T-186, T-188, T-189, T-190
Video screen grabs courtesy of Steadman Productions, Boston, MA

unit 1 *A busy schedule*

Before you watch

A Complete the sentences with the correct jobs. Then compare with a partner.

an artist

a doctor

a journalist

1. _____ studies chemistry.

2. _____ writes stories for newspapers.

3. _____ can draw and paint very well.

4. _____ makes creative things.

5. _____ interviews people a lot.

6. _____ takes a lot of science classes.

B **Pair work** Interview your partner. Take notes.

1. How many classes are you taking?

2. Why are you taking each class?

3. Do you like the subject(s) you are studying? Why or why not?

4. What job would you like to have someday?

C **Class activity** Share your information. Who is taking a lot of classes? Who is taking a fun class?

While you watch

A Circle the correct answers.

1. Danielle and Amy are _____.

    a. friends   b. neighbors   c. roommates

2. Danielle and April are studying _____.

    a. art   b. chemistry   c. journalism

3. Danielle and April are making a _____ for their class.

    a. picture   b. poster   c. video

4. Amy is taking _____ classes.

    a. five   b. six   c. seven

5. Danielle feels like she has a really _____ schedule.

    a. busy   b. easy   c. hard

B Check (✓) the correct answers.

	Amy	Danielle
1. Who thinks chemistry is difficult?	☐	☐
2. Who isn't hungry?	☐	☐
3. Who eats a lot before a big exam?	☐	☐
4. Who thinks art class looks stressful?	☐	☐
5. Who is learning to write stories for newspapers?	☐	☐
6. Who is preparing for medical school exams?	☐	☐

C Write T (true) or F (false). Correct the false sentences.

   Amy

1. ~~Danielle~~ has a big exam this week. ___*F*___

2. Amy drinks a lot of coffee. _____

3. When Danielle is nervous about something, she exercises. _____

4. Amy wants to be an artist. _____

5. Amy is late for class. _____

After you watch

A Why do you think Amy is so sleepy? Write your answers on the lines. Then compare with a partner.

> Amy is sleepy because she . . .

is preparing for medical   _____   _____

school exams.   _____ .   _____ .

B Group work Discuss the questions. Do any of you do the same things as Danielle or Amy?

- When you have a big exam, what do you do?
- If you're nervous about something, what do you do?
- What do you do if you feel sleepy in class?

An awful, terrible, embarrassing, really bad day!

Before you watch

A Look at the pictures. Complete the phrases with the correct verbs. Then compare with a partner.

get	lose	make	miss	spill	wait

1. _____ a drink   2. _____ an animation project   3. _____ in line

4. _____ a job   5. _____ a bad grade   6. _____ the bus

B Pair work When was the last time you did each thing in Part A? Are there some things you've never done? Tell your partner.

"I spilled coffee on my shirt this morning! I've never made an animation project."

While you watch

A What happened? Number the events from 1 to 9.

_____   April missed the bus to school.

___1___   April woke up late.

_____   April made an animation project.

_____   April's dog ate her homework.

_____   April went to the store for laundry detergent.

_____   April was late for her biology class.

_____   April sat next to Zach on the bus.

_____   April was late for work and lost her job.

April

B Circle the correct answers.

1. April spilled _____ on her shirt.

   a. orange juice   b. yogurt   c. coffee

2. April spilled _____ on Zach's shirt.

   a. orange juice   b. yogurt   c. coffee

3. Zach was _____ when April said she was sorry.

   a. angry   b. not amused   c. disgusted

4. The biology teacher's suggestion for April is to _____.

   a. do her homework again   b. come to class on time   c. give her dog some food

5. April didn't get the laundry detergent because _____.

   a. she didn't have enough money   b. there was a long line   c. there was none in the store

6. The one good thing that happened was that _____.

   a. Zach became April's boyfriend

   b. April found a new job after she lost her old one

   c. April had time to make an animation project for her art class

C Match the phrases to complete the sentences.

1. April was late for school _____

2. She was excited _____.

3. April was embarrassed when she lost her job _____.

4. She was late for work _____.

5. April got an "F" _____

a. because no one was sitting next to Zach.

b. because her dog ate her homework.

c. because there was a long line at the market.

d. because Zach was in the restaurant.

e. because her alarm clock didn't go off.

After you watch

A Pair work What was embarrassing about April's day? Do you know anyone who has had similar experiences to April? Tell your partner.

B Think about one very bad day in your life or the life of someone you know. Write three things about that day – two things that *really* happened, and one that *didn't* really happen.

1. _____

2. _____

3. _____

C Pair work Tell your partner about the bad day. Your partner guesses what didn't really happen. Take turns.

   A: I broke my elbow and lost my cell phone. Then someone stole my laptop.

   B: I don't think you really broke your elbow.

   A: That's not right. I *did* break my elbow, but no one really stole my laptop.

unit 3 *What's your personal style?*

Before you watch

A Complete the sentences with the correct words. Then compare with a partner.

bright	comfortable	conservative	fashionable	flashy	tacky

1. Many people think it is _____ to wear socks with sandals.

2. _____ clothing attracts attention and makes people stand out in a crowd.

3. People with a _____ style usually wear simple, plain clothes.

4. Orange and yellow are examples of _____ colors.

5. Models wear _____ clothing in magazines to help sell new items.

6. Most people think jeans, sneakers, and sweatshirts are _____.

B Pair work Make a list of ten words to describe clothing styles and fashion.
Then give examples of each one.

A: Glamorous *is another word to describe clothing styles and fashion.*

B: *Yes, it is. Who or what do you think is glamorous?*

A: *I think actors and actresses always look glamorous at award shows.*

B: *So do I.*

While you watch

A Check (✓) the correct answers. (More than one answer is possible.)

	Jim	Lola	Officer Palone
1. Who wears clothes that attract attention?	☐	☐	☐
2. Who thinks black is always fashionable?	☐	☐	☐
3. Who likes to wear comfortable clothes?	☐	☐	☐
4. Who usually wears many different colors?	☐	☐	☐
5. Who usually wears only two colors?	☐	☐	☐
6. Who usually wears only one color?	☐	☐	☐
7. Who used to wear flashy clothes?	☐	☐	☐
8. Who doesn't like flashy clothes?	☐	☐	☐

B Who is wearing each item in the video? Write E (Emi), J (Jim), L (Lola), or O (Officer Palone). (More than one answer is possible.)

1. a black jacket _____
2. a blue sweater _____
3. a gray shirt _____
4. a hat _____

5. a ponytail _____
6. a big bag _____
7. a red dress _____
8. a uniform _____

9. a white shirt _____
10. bracelets _____
11. earrings _____
12. sunglasses _____

C Correct the false sentences.

1. Jim wears a lot of blue and white clothing.
2. Jim likes to wear flashy and tacky clothes.
3. Lola doesn't like to stand out in a crowd.
4. Lola doesn't wear bright colors to work.
5. Officer Palone thinks his sunglasses are trendy.
6. Officer Palone's favorite color is red.

After you watch

A What was your clothing style five years ago? Complete the diagram with your own ideas. In the circle, write the style (retro? trendy? etc.). On the lines, write examples of some favorite clothes you used to wear.

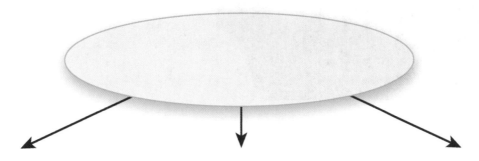

B Pair work Ask and answer questions about your diagrams. Did you use to wear any of the same things that you saw in the video?

A: *What was your clothing style?*

B: *Well, I used to wear a lot of black and white, like Jim in the video. I used to have some really cool black jeans. I wore them with a white T-shirt and a black leather jacket. I thought it was really trendy.*

4 *An interesting life*

Before you watch

A Complete the description with the correct words. Then compare with a partner.

| events | interview | newspapers | reporter | travel |

A foreign correspondent is a type of _____. Many foreign correspondents write stories for _____, but they may also work for TV or radio news stations. They usually have to _____ to many different countries for their job. They _____ many different people for their stories. They tell us about important people and _____ from around the world that have an impact on our history.

B Pair work Read the description again. Can you name any foreign correspondents? How do you find out about people and events from around the world? Tell your partner.

While you watch

A Circle the correct answers.

1. Danielle is making this video for her _____ class.

   a. journalism   b. world history   c. filmmaking

2. Irma was a _____ reporter.

   a. newspaper   b. TV   c. radio

3. She interviewed _____ in England.

   a. Queen Elizabeth   b. Princess Diana   c. Tony Blair

4. James Brown was a famous _____.

   a. hip-hop artist   b. actor   c. soul singer

5. Irma reported on a historical event in _____.

   a. England   b. Germany   c. the United States

B What does Irma say about James Brown? Write T (true) or F (false). Correct the false sentences.

1. James Brown was very polite and funny. _____

2. James Brown wasn't very hardworking. _____

3. James Brown used to practice an hour each day. _____

4. A lot of hip-hop artists have used his music. _____

5. She saw James Brown at the Apollo Theater in New York City. _____

C What does Irma say about the Berlin Wall? Check (✓) the correct answers.

☐ The fall of the Berlin Wall was the end of the Cold War.

☐ She took a piece of the wall home as a souvenir.

☐ People were so happy when it fell.

☐ People in East Berlin crossed the wall and celebrated with people in West Berlin.

☐ She won an award for her story.

☐ She lived in Berlin for five years after the wall fell.

After you watch

A Group work Irma described some memorable experiences. Discuss the questions.

• Which of Irma's experiences was your favorite? Why?

• Who is a famous person you would like to interview? Why?

"The Berlin Wall experience was my favorite. It was a big, historical event."

B Pair work Tell your partner about an interesting person you've met and a memorable experience you've had. Ask and answer questions for more information.

• Who was the person?

• Where did you meet him or her?

• Why was he or she interesting?

• When did you have this experience?

• Where were you?

• Why was it memorable?

"I met a famous jazz musician at a club. He was a talented saxophone player."

Travels with Nick and Ben: Yosemite National Park

Before you watch

A Label the pictures with the correct words. Then compare with a partner.

| a bear | a meadow | a mountain lion | a rattlesnake | a rock | a waterfall |

1. _____

2. _____

3. _____

4. _____

5. _____

6. _____

B Pair work Have you ever seen the animals or geographical features in Part A? Where can you find them? Tell your partner.

While you watch

A Read the sentences about Nick and Ben's trip to Yosemite National Park. Write T (true) or F (false).

1. They ate in a fancy restaurant. _____
2. They drove to the park. _____
3. They enjoyed the sunset. _____
4. They saw a bear. _____
5. They saw a mountain lion. _____
6. They saw very old trees. _____

7. They walked through a tree. _____
8. They went camping. _____
9. They went hiking. _____
10. They went rock climbing. _____
11. They went swimming. _____
12. They went to a spa. _____

B Match the phrases to complete the sentences.

1. El Capitán is _____.
2. Yosemite Falls is _____.
3. Bridalveil Falls is _____.
4. Mariposa Grove is _____.
5. Grizzly Giant is _____.
6. The California Tunnel Tree is _____.
7. A Sequoia is _____.

a. a beautiful waterfall.
b. the highest waterfall in North America.
c. a tree that people can walk through.
d. the oldest Sequoia tree in Mariposa Grove.
e. a forest of Sequoia trees.
f. a type of tree.
g. a huge rock.

C Who says it? Check (✓) the correct answers.

	Ben	Nick
1. "Yosemite National Park – the most beautiful place on earth."	☐	☐
2. "Yosemite National Park – the most dangerous place on earth."	☐	☐
3. "I saw a rattlesnake while I was walking on the road."	☐	☐
4. "Look at that! Don't you think that looks dangerous?"	☐	☐
5. "It was exciting and challenging!"	☐	☐
6. "It was stressful. It was frightening. And it was wet!"	☐	☐
7. "Water can't hurt you!"	☐	☐
8. "I left the food in the car."	☐	☐

After you watch

A **Pair work** How would you describe Nick and Ben's trip? Would you like to go to Yosemite National Park? Why or why not? Discuss your ideas.

B **Group work** Discuss these questions about trips you've taken.
- What was the most exciting trip you've ever taken? Where did you go?
- What was your favorite trip? What did you do?
- What was the worst trip you've ever taken? What was so bad about it?
- Have you ever been in a dangerous situation on vacation? What happened?

C **Class activity** Tell the class the most interesting information or stories from your group discussion.

The time of your life

Before you watch

A Check (✓) the problems you have managing your time. Then compare with a partner.

☐ committing to too much work
☐ doing other people's work
☐ doing too many favors for other people
☐ finding time for your personal life
☐ finding time to be with your family
☐ keeping your home clean

☐ planning your weekly schedule
☐ remembering important things
☐ saying no to other people
☐ studying for exams
☐ taking on too many school projects
☐ working and going to school

Other: _____

B Pair work Who do you talk to when you're stressed out? Does anyone help you manage your time? Tell your partner.

While you watch

A Check (✓) the correct answers.

	Wendy	Nick	Soon-mi
1. Who can't find a list of things to do this weekend?	☐	☐	☐
2. Who commits to too much work?	☐	☐	☐
3. Who does a lot of other people's work?	☐	☐	☐
4. Who doesn't have time to finish the show?	☐	☐	☐
5. Who has to pay bills this weekend?	☐	☐	☐
6. Who is busy all the time?	☐	☐	☐
7. Who is late for the show?	☐	☐	☐
8. Who is too busy this weekend?	☐	☐	☐
9. Who needs to study for an exam?	☐	☐	☐
10. Who takes on too many projects at school?	☐	☐	☐

B Circle the correct answers.

1. Wendy's show is called _____.

    a. TV Time   b. The Time Saver   c. The Time of Your Life

2. Nick needs to shop for _____ this weekend.

    a. groceries   b. clothes   c. school supplies

3. Wendy tells Nick to _____.

    a. call his mother   b. breathe slowly and deeply   c. cancel the party

4. Wendy's advice to Nick is to _____.

    a. make a list   b. go to the movies   c. pay his bills first

5. Wendy tells Soon-mi to _____.

    a. do things one at a time   b. help her classmates   c. learn to say no

6. Wendy _____ Chris's question.

    a. answers   b. likes   c. never hears

C Write T (true) or F (false).

1. Wendy is very good at managing her own time. _____

2. Wendy doesn't have any children. _____

3. Nick is having a birthday party for someone this weekend. _____

4. If Nick follows Wendy's advice, he probably won't go to the movies this weekend. _____

5. If Soon-mi follows Wendy's advice, she'll probably do the grocery shopping for her roommate. _____

6. Soon-mi learns to say no. _____

After you watch

A Pair work Do you ever have the same problems as Wendy, Nick, or Soon-mi? Do you know other people who do? How do you (or they) manage them? Tell your partner.

B Pair work Make a list of five things you plan to do this weekend. Then share them with a partner.

1. _____

2. _____

3. _____

4. _____

5. _____

C Pair work Now imagine that you have time to do only three things on your list. Which two plans will you decide *not* to do? Why? Tell your partner.

Four Corners

Jack C. Richards · David Bohlke

with Kathryn O'Dell

3A

Workbook

CAMBRIDGE
UNIVERSITY PRESS

Contents

Credits

Education

A *I'm taking six classes.*

1 Look at the pictures. Write the correct school subjects.

1. c*hemistry*_____

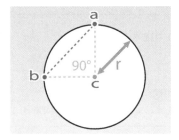

2. g_____

3. w_____

g_____

4. m_____

5. h_____

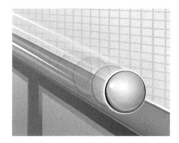

6. p_____

7. b_____

8. a_____

9. a_____

2 Complete the sentences with the correct school subjects from Exercise 1.

1. Sandra's favorite classes are science classes: _____*chemistry*_____ ,
_____ , and _____ .

2. John has two math classes: _____ and _____ .

3. Leo's favorite classes are in the arts: _____ and _____ .

4. Mi-hee is taking two social studies classes: _____
and _____ .

3 Check (✓) the correct sentences. Rewrite the incorrect sentences with the correct forms of the verbs. Use the simple present or the present continuous.

1. ☐ Dina reads her email right now.

   Dina is reading her email right now.

2. ☐ Tim is knowing a lot about biology.

   _____

3. ☐ Mateo and Alicia are taking a dance class together.

   _____

4. ☐ I'm wanting to study in Australia in the summer.

   _____

5. ☐ What is the word "engineer" meaning?

   _____

6. ☐ Do you go to class right now?

   _____

7. ☐ They don't remember the answers for the history test.

   _____

8. ☐ This homework isn't seeming difficult.

   _____

4 Look at the schedule. Complete the sentences with the correct forms of *work*. Use the simple present or the present continuous.

Officemart Summer Schedule			
Name	**Fridays**	**Saturdays**	**Sundays**
Marcia	2:00 p.m. – 8:00 p.m.	9:00 a.m. – 3:00 p.m.	✗
Leo	10:00 a.m. – 5:00 p.m.	9:00 a.m. – 5:00 p.m.	12:00 p.m. – 4:00 p.m.
Paul	✗	2:00 p.m. – 7:30 p.m.	✗

1. Marcia and Leo _____ work _____ on Fridays and Saturdays.

2. It's Sunday, and Marcia and Paul _____ .

3. It's 11:00 a.m. on Friday. Leo _____ .

4. It's 3:30 p.m. on Saturday. Leo and Paul _____ right now.

5. Leo _____ on Sunday afternoons.

6. Paul _____ on Fridays.

7. It's 6:00 p.m. on Friday. Leo _____ right now.

8. Marcia and Leo _____ on Saturday evenings.

5 Complete the text messages with the correct forms of the verbs in parentheses. Use the simple present or the present continuous.

J.Monk78: Hi, Shelly. What _are you doing_ (do) right now?
1

SLP1980: Hey, Jin-sung. I _____ (write) to you! ☺
2

J.Monk78: Very funny! _____ you _____ (study) for the chemistry test?
3   3

SLP1980: Yes, I am. Linda and I _____ (read) the teacher's notes online.
4

J.Monk78: I _____ (not / understand) those notes at all.
5

SLP1980: _____ you _____ (want) some help?
6   6

J.Monk78: Yes, please!

Emmie: Hey, Kate. What classes _____ you _____ (have) on Fridays?
7   7

KateM: I _____ (have) algebra in the mornings and geometry in the afternoons.
8

Emmie: What time _____ (be) your geometry class?
9

KateM: At 2:00. Wait . . . my sister _____ (call) me . . .
10

KateM: OK. I'm back. My sister _____ (shop) right now. Let's go to the mall.
11

Emmie: OK, but I _____ (work) right now. How about at 11:30?
12

KateM: Great! Let's meet in front of Los Zapatos Shoe Store.

---

6 Answer the questions with your own information. Write complete sentences.

Example: _I'm taking English, physics, and music._

1. What classes are you taking? _____

2. When do you study? _____

3. How often do you have English classes? _____

4. Where do you usually do your homework? _____

5. What school subjects do you like? _____

6. What school subjects do you hate? _____

7. What are you doing right now? _____

8. Where are you sitting? _____

B You're not allowed to . . .

1 Complete the chart with the sentences from the box.

✓You can't use your cell phone in the office.	You need to have lunch at that time.
You have to come to work by 9:00.	You're not permitted to eat in your office.
You must always wear a suit to work.	You're not allowed to write emails to friends.

Prohibition	Obligation
You can't use your cell phone in the office.	

2 Complete the conversation with the correct sentences from the box in Exercise 1.

Ms. Jones: Welcome to Akron Accounting. This is your new office. Do you have any questions?

Mr. Okada: Yes. Can I make personal phone calls at work?

Ms. Jones: No, I'm sorry. *You can't use your cell phone in the office.*
1
You can make personal calls at lunch.

Mr. Okada: OK. What time is lunch?

Ms. Jones: It's from 1:00 to 2:00.

_____ .
2

Mr. Okada: Can I have lunch at my desk?

Ms. Jones: No, I'm sorry. _____ .
3
You can have lunch in our café, or you can go out to eat. There are a lot of good restaurants on Pine Street.

Mr. Okada: OK. Thanks. Is there anything else I need to know?

Ms. Jones: Yes. _____ .
4
We try to dress for business here.

Mr. Okada: No problem.

1 Look at the pictures. Complete the puzzle with the feelings and emotions you see. What's the mystery word?

 1.

 2.

 3.

		¹T	H	I	R	S	T	Y
	2							
3								
4								
5								
6								

 4.

 5.

 6.

2 Complete the sentences with the correct words from the box.

hungry	jealous	scared	✓thirsty	upset

1. Miguel wants some water. He's _____ *thirsty* _____ .

2. Carla didn't eat lunch today, and now she's very _____ .

3. John's team didn't win their soccer game. He's extremely _____ about it.

4. Paula is an actress. Mariana wants to be an actress, but right now she's a waitress. She's _____ of Paula.

5. When Peggy came home last night, her front door was open. She was _____ and called the police.

3 Complete the conversation with *if* and the correct words from the box.

I have a job interview	I'm prepared	there's a website
I'm nervous	she's home	✓you're nervous

Carmen: Hey, Danielle. What do you do

if you're nervous ?
₁

Danielle: _____ about
₂
something, I try not to think about it.

Carmen: Well, I have a job interview tomorrow, and

I have to think about it!

Danielle: Hmm . . . _____ ,
₃
I usually prepare before I go. It really helps.

Carmen: How do you prepare?

Danielle: _____ , I read about the place online.
₄

Carmen: That's a good idea.

Danielle: Yes. I also practice the interview with my sister _____ .
₅

Carmen: I can try that with my brother. What about during the interview?

Danielle: _____ , I usually don't get nervous. Good luck!
₆

4 Combine the sentences into one. Use *when*. Write it in two ways.

1. Emma has a test. → She studies a lot.

   When Emma has a test, she studies a lot.

   Emma studies a lot when she has a test.

2. I get bad news. → I get upset.

   _____

   _____

3. Jordan gets up early in the morning. → He is sleepy.

   _____

   _____

4. My sister is busy. → She doesn't call me.

   _____

   _____

5. Lorena and Jessie have a soccer game. → They get nervous.

   _____

   _____

5 Write sentences in the zero conditional. Use the words in the chart.

Condition	Main clause	If / When
1. Tonya's sister / go to a party	Tonya / always / get jealous	when
2. Greg / be lonely	he / often / call a friend	when
3. I / get scared	I / always / call my brother	if
4. Kyle and Rick / be busy	they / sometimes / not eat	if
5. Leticia / get angry	she / usually / not say anything	when
6. I / be late for work	I / usually / say I'm sorry	if

1. _When Tonya's sister goes to a party, Tonya always gets jealous._

2. _____

3. _____

4. _____

5. _____

6. _____

6 Write questions with the words in parentheses. Use *What* and the zero conditional.

1. (Charlie / do / if / be sleepy)   _What does Charlie do if he's sleepy?_

2. (you / do / when / get upset)   _____

3. (Frank and Julie / do / if / get angry)   _____

4. (you / do / if / be hungry)   _____

5. (you and your friends / do / when / be thirsty)   _____

6. (Annette / do / when / feel nervous)   _____

7 Answer the questions with your own information. Write complete sentences with the zero conditional.

Example: _When I'm nervous about a test, I study really hard._

1. What do you do when you're nervous about a test?   _____

2. What do you do if you're sleepy in class?   _____

3. How do you feel when you're too busy?   _____

4. What do you do when you're lonely?   _____

5. What do you drink if you're thirsty?   _____

6. What do you say when you're angry with a friend?   _____

D Alternative education

1 Read the article. Answer the questions.

1. Who works for a magazine? _____

2. Who works for an engineer? _____

Work-Study Programs in High School

Many high schools in the United States have work-study programs. In their last year of high school, some students have a job for part of the day as one of their "classes." Some of these students make money and some don't, but all of them learn important things about having a job and being a good worker. Many people think that when students learn outside of the classroom in a real job, they prepare for life after high school. Work-study programs can really help students get a job or get into college.

There are many types of work-study programs. Most of the students work in offices, but not all of them do. Some students fix cars, and others work outside with environmental engineers. Big businesses, like computer companies and banks, often work with high schools to create work-study opportunities for students as well.

Raul Gomez usually goes to school from 9:00 a.m. to 4:00 p.m., but this year he works for a magazine from 7:00 a.m. to 11:00 a.m. He says, "I learn important things in my work-study program. I must be at work on time. And if I miss a day, they don't pay me!" At work, he reads stories and fixes spelling and grammar mistakes. He says, "At work, I use what I learn in my English class. And now I think that someday, I might want to write for a magazine or a newspaper."

Raul Gomez at his work-study job

Annie Miller works for an engineer in her work-study program. They design and help make bridges, roads, and buildings. She says, "It's great! I love learning math in school, but at work, I use algebra and geometry in the real world!"

Not all high schools offer work-study programs. But most of the schools that have them think they are a big success.

2 Read the text again. Then write T (true), F (false), or NI (no information).

1. Work-study programs started in the United States. __NI__

2. Some students get money in work-study programs. _____

3. Work-study programs rarely help students start their careers or further their education. _____

4. Raul works at his job in the morning. _____

5. Annie likes science classes. _____

6. Not many of the work-study programs are a success. _____

Personal stories

A What were you doing?

1 Put the letters in the correct order to make adverbs. Complete the sentences.

(y u o u t r n l f t a n e)

1. I was having a great day on Tuesday. Then, ___*unfortunately*___, I left my bag at a restaurant.

(l l i c y u k)

2. _____ , someone found it.

(l y f e t o a n u t r)

3. And _____ , my cell phone was in the bag.

(l s y r u i n s g i p r)

4. _____ , the person who found it called my home phone.

(a z n i g a y m l)

5. _____ , the person was David, a boy I went to school with when I was six! We made plans to meet at a café.

(y e s t a r g l n)

6. _____ , David looked the same! We ate lunch and talked a lot.

(s n u e y d d l)

7. Then David got a phone call, and he left the café _____ .

(s a y l d)

8. _____ , I never saw him again.

2 What were they doing when the lights went out? Write sentences with the past continuous forms of the verbs.

1. (Mi-na / read / a book)

   Mi-na was reading a book.

2. (Martin / wash / the dishes)

   _____

3. (Brad and Kate / watch / TV)

   _____

4. (I / talk / to Tom / on the phone)

   _____

5. (Laura / play / video games)

   _____

6. (Mr. and Mrs. Jones / eat / dinner)

   _____

3 Complete the sentences with *when* and the words in parentheses. Use the simple past forms of the verbs.

1. (their friends / arrive)

   Jane and Paul were making dinner on Friday *when their friends arrived* _____ .

2. (his brother / call)

   Martin was driving to the store _____ .

3. (the electricity / go off)

   What were you doing yesterday _____ ?

4. (Jill / send me / a text message)

   _____ , I was talking to Tom on my cell phone.

5. (the ambulance / come)

   What were they doing _____ ?

6. (the storm / begin)

   _____ , I was walking home from work.

4 Complete the conversation with the correct forms of the simple past or the past continuous of the verbs in parentheses.

Rick: Hi, Lisa. What _____*were*_____ you _____*doing*_____ (do)
         when the electricity _____*went*_____ (go) off?
              2

Lisa: Unfortunately, I _____ (work)
                              3
         on the computer! I couldn't finish my work. What
         _____ you _____ (do)?
              4   4

Rick: Oh, I _____ (sleep) when
                   5
         everything _____ (go) dark.
                           6
         I didn't even know what happened.

Lisa: Really? It was only 7:30 p.m.

Rick: Well, I _____ (take) a nap in the living room. I think I slept
                    7
         for a long time. When I _____ (wake) up, it was really dark.
                                       8
         So I just went to bed. While everyone _____ (have) problems,
                                                        9
         I _____ (sleep)!
              10

5 Complete the story with the verbs in the box. Use the past continuous or the simple past.

✓cook	go	make	stand	turn
fall	hear	see	try	

Terry and Wendy _____*were cooking*_____ in the kitchen when the electricity suddenly
                              1
_____ off. Unfortunately, while Terry _____ to find
        2   3
a light, he _____ down. He _____ a loud noise.
                    4   5
When Wendy _____ the noise, she _____ by the
                       6   7
window. While she _____ around, she _____
                           8   9
something move outside the window. What was it?

6 Answer the questions with your own information. Write complete sentences.

Example: _I took biology, history of China, and English last year._

1. What classes did you take last year?   _____

2. What were you saying the last time you spoke? _____

3. Where did you eat breakfast today?   _____

4. What did you do last night?   _____

5. What were you doing at 6:00 a.m. today?   _____

6. What were you doing when class started?   _____

B Guess what!

1 Write A (announcing news) or C (closing a conversation).

1. Listen, I've got to run. __C__

2. You'll never guess what happened! _____

3. Sorry, I have to go. _____

4. Hey, I need to get going. _____

5. Guess what! _____

6. Did you hear what happened? _____

2 Complete the conversations with the sentences from Exercise 1. Sometimes more than one answer is possible. Use each sentence once.

A. **Jim:** Hello, Pat. _Did you hear what_
1
happened?

    Pat: No, I didn't.

    Jim: There was an accident on Main Street.

    Pat: That's terrible!

    Jim: Yes, it is. Fortunately, everyone is OK.

    _____ .
2

    Pat: OK. Bye.

a car accident

B. **Annie:** Hey, Tonya! _____ !
1

    Tonya: What?

    Annie: Martin got a promotion, and he's moving to Canada.

    Tonya: That's great.

    Annie: I know. _____ . I have a meeting
2
in a few minutes.

    Tonya: No problem. Call me later!

C. **Beth:** Hi, Dan. _____ !
1

    Dan: What?

    Beth: Our soccer team won the competition.

    Dan: That's fantastic! _____ . I have
2
class now. But congratulations!

    Beth: That's OK. Thanks. See you tomorrow.

C *I was really frightened!*

1 Put the letters in the correct order to make verbs that describe reactions.

1. i e t e c x   _____*excite*_____   5. g e t h f i r n   _____

2. d u s s g i t   _____   6. a u e s m   _____

3. s o u n f c e   _____   7. e c n l a g h l e   _____

4. i t t n r s e e   _____   8. s m a e s a r b r   _____

2 Complete the conversations with the correct forms of the verbs in Exercise 1.
Use the simple present.

1. **Nancy:** Hey, Karl. Did you do the homework for math class?

   Karl: No, I didn't. Geometry _____*confuses*_____ me. I don't understand it.

2. **Po:** Jill. Try this sushi.

   Jill: No, thanks. Fish _____ me! I hate it!

3. **Larry:** My brother talks too loudly. He really _____ me when
   he's with my friends.

   David: It's not so bad. He's very friendly.

4. **Tom:** What _____ you, Seth?

   Seth: Horror movies! I get really scared when I watch them.

5. **Ted:** Do you like animated movies?

   Lea: Yes, they usually _____ me. I think they're funny.

6. **Ahmet:** Chemistry _____ me, but I think physics is boring.

   Andrea: Really? I think physics is interesting.

7. **Miho:** What do you want to do this weekend? Anything exciting?

   Karen: Well, the idea of going to Chicago for the weekend _____ me!

8. **Eva:** You're pretty good at sports, Tim. What kind of sport _____ you?

   Tim: Golf, I guess. It's a lot more difficult than it seems.

3 Complete the sentences with the present participles (*-ing*) or past participles (*-ed*) of the verbs in parentheses.

1. Amusement parks are _____exciting_____ (excite).

2. Can you help me? This physics problem is _____ (confuse).

3. I want a new job because my work is too easy. I don't feel _____ (challenge).

4. I don't think your problem is _____ (embarrass). A lot of people talk fast when they're nervous.

5. I'm _____ (frighten) by our neighbor's dog! It's big and extremely loud.

6. I'm not _____ (interest) in math, but I love science.

7. I don't think video games are _____ (amuse), but many teenagers like them.

8. My brother is _____ (disgust) by reality shows, but I'd like to be on one!

4 Circle the correct words to complete the conversation.

Paul: Hi, Wendy. Have you ever read *Life of Pi*? You know . . . that story about a boy who is on the ocean in a boat with a tiger.

Wendy: Yes, I have. I liked it, but I thought some parts with the tiger were **disgusted** / (**disgusting**)
1

Paul: Really? I thought it was **frightened** / **frightening**, but I was **excited** / **exciting** when I read it.
2   3

Wendy: Well, yes, it was **excited** / **exciting**. But after a while, I think Pi was probably **bored** / **boring** on that boat. He was on it for 227 days!
4   5

Paul: Oh, I don't think so. I bet life on that boat wasn't **bored** / **boring** at all! I loved how he became friends with the tiger. That was really **interested** / **interesting**.
6   7

Wendy: Yeah. That part was **amused** / **amusing**, I guess, but it didn't seem like real life.
8

Paul: Maybe not, but I think the story shows that sometimes life is **challenged** / **challenging**.
9

Wendy: Yeah, you're right. And I guess the end was **surprised** / **surprising**.
10

Paul: Um, well . . . now I'm **embarrassed** / **embarrassing**. To be honest, I didn't finish the book!
11

5 Read Ron's online survey. Then complete the sentences about Ron's opinions.

We want to hear from you!

1 What kind of music are you interested in?
☑ rock ☐ jazz ☐ blues ☑ techno

2 What do you think of concerts?
☑ exciting ☐ boring ☑ amusing

3 Who are you embarrassed by?
☐ your parents ☑ your brothers and sisters ☐ your friends

4 What do think about technology?
☑ confusing ☑ challenging ☐ easy

5 What kinds of foods do you think are disgusting?
☑ fish ☐ meat ☐ fruit ☑ vegetables

1. Ron is _____*interested*_____ in *rock and techno music*_____ .

2. He thinks _____*concerts*_____ are _____ .

3. He is _____ by _____ .

4. He thinks _____ is _____ .

5. He thinks _____ are _____ .

6 Write sentences about your opinions with a participial adjective from the box.

Example: _I think horror movies are amusing._ or _I'm frightened by horror movies._

amused / amusing	disgusted / disgusting	frightened / frightening
bored / boring	embarrassed / embarrassing	interested / interesting
challenged / challenging	excited / exciting	surprised / surprising
confused / confusing		

1. horror movies: _____

2. history classes: _____

3. the news: _____

4. reading books: _____

5. reality shows: _____

6. math: _____

D How embarrassing!

1 Read the email. Then check (✓) the correct adjectives.

1. The hotel is _____ .
   ☐ interesting   ☐ dirty   ☐ embarrassing

2. The Japanese street names are _____ .
   ☐ amusing   ☐ challenging   ☐ disgusting

3. Angela did two things that were _____ .
   ☐ traditional   ☐ interesting   ☐ embarrassing

Hi George,

I'm having an amazing time in Japan! I'm in Kyoto visiting a lot of interesting places. I'm staying in a *ryokan*. It's a traditional Japanese hotel. It's really interesting. The hotel is part of a man and woman's home. Their names are Mr. and Mrs. Ito. I have breakfast by myself at the *ryokan*, and I eat lunch in the city, but I have dinner with the family in their part of the house. And their daughter brings me tea in the evening before I go to bed! (I feel like a very important person!)

I'm learning a lot about life in Japan, but I'm also doing some embarrassing things by mistake! In the *ryokan*, you take off your shoes before you go in the house so that the floor doesn't get dirty. You leave your shoes outside the door. On my first day, I took off my shoes, but I did it in my bedroom. I walked through the house first, and I got the floor dirty. How embarrassing! I hope Mr. and Mrs. Ito weren't disgusted with me. But they are nice and very friendly, and now I remember to take off my shoes before I come in the house.

I was also embarrassed while I was traveling around the city yesterday. I don't speak Japanese, but I speak Spanish. When I asked for directions, no one understood me! I was pronouncing the street names like Spanish words. They're very difficult to say! But it's easy to get around in Kyoto. The buses and trains are extremely modern and clean. Tomorrow I'm going to an art museum. I'm going to practice pronouncing the museum name and the street name in Japanese tonight!

It's really fun here. I don't want to go back home!

Your friend,

Angela

2 Read the text again. Then answer the questions. Write complete sentences.

1. Where is Angela staying in Kyoto? _____

2. Who gives Angela tea? _____

3. What two embarrassing things did Angela do? _____

4. What is Angela's opinion of the buses and trains? _____

5. What is Angela doing tomorrow? _____

Style and fashion

A *Fashion trends*

1 Look at the pictures. Complete the puzzle with fashion words.

Across

4.

5.

7.

8.

Down

1.

2.

3.

6.

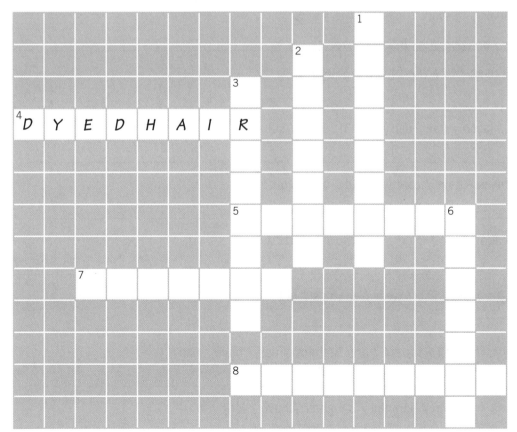

2 Cross out the fashion word that doesn't belong in each list.

1. **Clothing:**   ~~a bracelet~~   a leather jacket   a uniform

2. **Hairstyles:**   a ponytail   dyed hair   sandals

3. **Jewelry:**   earrings   a bracelet   glasses

4. **Eyewear:**   contact lenses   earrings   glasses

5. **Shoes:**   sandals   a uniform   high heels

3 Put the words in the correct order to make sentences.

1. high heels / to work / used / I / to / wear / .

   I used to wear high heels to work.

2. wear / used / to / wig / My / mother / a / .

   _____

3. every / Jason / day / use / didn't / wear / suits / to / .

   _____

4. to / lenses / have / contact / Did / use / you / ?

   _____

5. on vacation / We / used / buy / to / T-shirts / .

   _____

6. to / Katia / Did / use / wear / earrings / big / ?

   _____

7. dyed / to / didn't / Sandra / and Bethany / use / have / hair / .

   _____

8. used / a / My / to / ponytail / daughter / have / long / .

   _____

4 Circle the correct words to complete each conversation.

1. **A:** Did you _____ to have dyed hair?

   B: No, I _____ , but I do now.

   a. use, did   (b.) use, didn't   c. used, did   d. used, didn't

2. **A:** Did Leo _____ to wear a bracelet?

   B: Yes, he _____ ! But now he doesn't wear any jewelry.

   a. used, did   b. used, didn't   c. use, did   d. use, didn't

3. **A:** Where _____ Kelly and Margie use to shop?

   B: They _____ to shop at the mall.

   a. didn't, use   b. didn't, used   c. did, use   d. did, used

4. **A:** What kinds of clothes did Jake _____ to wear?

   B: He _____ to wear T-shirts and baggy jeans.

   a. use, use   b. used, use   c. use, used   d. used, used

5. **A:** Did you _____ to wear glasses?

   B: Yes. I didn't _____ to wear contact lenses.

   a. use, use   b. used, use   c. use, used   d. used, used

5 Look at Emma's information. Then write sentences with the words in parentheses. Use *used to* or *didn't use to*.

What did you use to wear?

	1970s	1980s	1990s	2000s
baggy jeans	✓	✗	✗	✓
tight jeans	✗	✓	✓	✓
bright T-shirts	✓	✓	✗	✗
high heels	✗	✗	✓	✓
big earrings	✓	✓	✓	✗

1. (bright T-shirts / the 1970s)   _Emma used to wear bright T-shirts in the 1970s._

2. (high heels / the 1970s)   _She didn't_ _____

3. (baggy jeans / the 1980s)   _____

4. (tight jeans / the 1980s)   _____

5. (big earrings / the 1990s)   _____

6. (big earrings / the 2000s)   _____

B *Does this come in . . . ?*

1 Write the conversation in the correct order.

Can I help you?	Oh, thanks! Um, do you have this in brown?
✓ Excuse me.	They're here, behind you.
No, I'm sorry. It only comes in black.	Yes. Where can I find the leather jackets?

Renaldo: _Excuse me._____

Clerk: _____

Renaldo: _____

Clerk: _____

Renaldo: _____

Clerk: _____

2 Write a conversation for each picture with the words in the box and your own ideas. Use the conversation in Exercise 1 as a model.

Can I get this in . . . ?	Does this come in . . . ?
Could you tell me where the . . . are?	Where are the . . . ?

1. **Debbie:** Excuse me.

   Clerk: _____ ?

   Debbie: Yes. _____ ?

   Clerk: _____ .

   Debbie: Oh, thanks! _____ in red?

   Clerk: No, I'm sorry. _____ .

2. **Ichiro:** _____ .

   Clerk: _____ ?

   Ichiro: Yes. _____ ?

   Clerk: _____ .

   Ichiro: Oh, thanks! _____ in blue?

   Clerk: Yes. _____ .

The latest look

1 Read about the types of clothes. Then write the fashion word that matches each type.

1. clothes that people like right now but might not like next year: _t_ _r_ _e_ _n_ _d_ _y_

2. clothes that are the style that people want or like: __ __ __ __ __ __ __ __ __ __ __

3. clothes that used to be what people liked: __ __ __ - __ __ __ __ __ __ __ __ __

4. new clothes that look like old styles (in a good way): __ __ __ __ __

5. clothes that look expensive and exciting (in a good way): __ __ __ __ __ __ __ __ __

6. usually cheap clothes of bad quality or bad style: __ __ __ __ __

7. clothes that look very strange: __ __ __ __ __

8. clothes that attract a lot of attention because they're bright: __ __ __ __ __ __

2 Look at the pictures. Complete the sentences with your own opinions. Use words from the box. Not all the words will be used.

fashionable	glamorous	retro	trendy
flashy	old-fashioned	tacky	weird

Example: *Her dress is fashionable.* or *Her dress is flashy.*

1. Her dress is _____ .

2. Her shoes are _____ .

3. Her sunglasses are _____ .

4. His shirt is _____ .

5. His pants are _____ .

6. His hat is _____ .

3 Rewrite the sentences. Replace *that* with *which* or *who*.

1. I don't like clothes that are trendy.

   I don't like clothes which are trendy.

2. Tonya is the kind of person that buys things for other people.

   _____

3. I like the kind of store that has a lot of sales.

   _____

4. Is Jason someone that follows fashion trends?

   _____

5. We prefer salesclerks that give us their opinions.

   _____

6. Carla prefers shoes that are not high heels.

   _____

7. Is there a store in the mall that sells sunglasses?

   _____

8. Greg and Roberto are people that always wear retro clothes.

   _____

4 Complete the conversation with *which* or *who*.

Emily: Mom, what is a fashion designer?

Mom: It's a person _____*who*_____ makes new
                                    1
clothing styles.

Emily: And what is a tailor shop?

Mom: It's a store _____ has tailors.
                                 2

Emily: OK . . . but what's a tailor?

Mom: Well, a tailor is a person _____
                                                    3
makes or fixes clothes.

Emily: Really? OK. And what does a stylist do?

Mom: That's a person _____ helps actors look good.
                                        4

Emily: Thanks, Mom!

Mom: Why are you asking me all these questions?

Emily: I found this magazine _____ is about fashion. I'm taking a quiz in it.
                                             5

Mom: You mean, *I'm* taking a quiz in it!

5 Read the question. Then complete the response with *who, that,* or *which* and the correct forms of the verbs and other words in parentheses.

1. **A:** Who is Ms. Young?

   B: She is the chemistry teacher _who wears_

   flashy clothes . (wear / flashy clothes)

2. **A:** Does Marvin buy all types of clothes?

   B: No, he doesn't. He usually buys clothes

   _____ .

   (be / fashionable)

3. **A:** What kind of malls do you like?

   B: I like malls _____ .

   (have / a lot of stores with trendy clothes)

4. **A:** Who is Jennifer X?

   B: She's a singer _____ .

   (wear / weird clothes at her concerts)

5. **A:** Who is Jacques?

   B: He's that famous designer _____ .

   (make / retro clothing)

6. **A:** What is *Viv*?

   B: It's a website _____ .

   (sell / old-fashioned jewelry)

6 Complete the sentences with your own information.

Example: _Black is a color that I wear a lot._

1. _____ is a color that I wear a lot.

2. _____ is a person who has a style that I really like.

3. _____ is a magazine or website that people read for information about fashion.

4. _____ is a clothing style that is trendy right now.

5. _____ is a place that sells clothes that I like to wear.

6. _____ is someone who wears clothes that are fashionable.

D Views on fashion

1 Read the article. Then match the two parts of each sentence.

1. Coco Chanel was a woman _____   a. who made the first jeans.

2. Levi Strauss was the man _____   b. who wrote about fashion.

3. Richard Blackwell was a person _____   c. who designed hats and clothing for women.

People Who Changed Fashion

Coco Chanel was a French fashion designer who changed fashion for women. She started making glamorous hats in her apartment. Then a famous actress wore Chanel's hats in a play, and suddenly many women wanted her hats. So Chanel started a business and opened a hat store in 1913. In the early 1900s, women used to wear uncomfortable skirts, but Chanel wanted to be comfortable. She often wore men's pants, jackets, and ties. She started making comfortable and fashionable clothing for women. She made pants and women's suits that were comfortable and trendy, and she began selling them in her store. By 1919, she opened a larger store and was famous in France and other parts of the world. She changed women's clothing, and she inspired other designers.

Levi Strauss had a clothing store in California in the 1870s. His store sold work clothes for men. At that time, working men wore pants that ripped or tore a lot. Strauss worked together with the tailor Jacob Davis to make better pants that were strong and that a man could wear for a long time. They made the pants with a heavy cloth called denim. At that time, there was another heavy cloth called jean. People started to call the denim pants *jeans*. Jeans used to be for work, but they became trendy in the 1950s when teenagers started wearing them. Now many people wear them, even when they aren't working.

Richard Blackwell was an American designer who wrote about fashion. In 1960, he wrote a "Ten Worst-Dressed Women" list in a magazine. People didn't use to talk badly about famous people's clothes, but Blackwell wrote about actresses who wore clothes that he thought were ugly or weird. Today, there are many TV shows with people who give opinions about the clothes that actors and actresses are wearing these days. There are also many websites that have "Worst-Dressed" lists about celebrities.

2 Read the article again. Answer the questions. Write complete sentences.

1. What was the first item of clothing Coco Chanel made?   *She made hats.*

2. Why did Chanel sometimes wear men's clothing?   _____

3. Why did Levi Strauss make pants from denim?   _____

4. Who made jeans trendy?   _____

5. Who did Richard Blackwell write about?   _____

Interesting lives

A Have you ever been on TV?

1 Look at the pictures. Check (✓) the correct sentence for each picture.

1. ✓ I often get seasick.
   ☐ I often lose my phone.
   ☐ I often win an award.

2. ☐ I moved to a new city last week.
   ☐ I was on TV last week.
   ☐ I acted in a play last week.

3. ☐ I met a famous person in New York.
   ☐ I broke my arm in New York.
   ☐ I was on TV in New York.

4. ☐ I got seasick at work.
   ☐ I broke my arm at work.
   ☐ I won an award at work.

5. ☐ I used to act in plays.
   ☐ I used to be on TV.
   ☐ I used to win awards.

6. ☐ We're meeting a famous person.
   ☐ We're acting in a play.
   ☐ We're moving to a new city.

2 Complete the chart. Write the past participles. Then write R (regular) or I (irregular).

Base Form	Past Participle	Regular or Irregular
1. lose		
2. be		
3. act		
4. chat		
5. see		
6. win		
7. have		
8. go		

Base Form	Past Participle	Regular or Irregular
9. try		
10. break		
11. happen		
12. do		
13. meet		
14. move		
15. eat		
16. get		

3 Complete the conversation with the present perfect forms of the verbs in parentheses. For answers to questions, use short answers.

Joe: Hey, Marta. _____*Have*_____ you ever
     1
_____*been*_____ (be) on TV?
     1

Marta: Yes, I _____*have*_____ . I was interviewed
     2
about the Japanese language school I went to
in Tokyo. Hey, _____ you ever
     3
_____ (visit) Japan?
     3

Joe: No, I _____ .
     4

Marta: It's great. I studied there for a month.

Joe: What did you like the best?

Marta: The food! _____ you ever _____ (try) sushi?
     5   5

Joe: Yes, I _____ . I like Japanese food. I also like Korean
     6
food. _____ you ever _____ (try) Korean food?
     7   7

Marta: Yes. I _____ . A few times. _____ you ever
     8   9
_____ (go) to South Korea?
     9

Joe: No, I _____ . But my sister _____ (be) there. She went to Seoul.
     10   11

Marta: I hear they have good food at the markets in Seoul. _____ she ever
     12
_____ (eat) at a night market?
     12

Joe: Yes, she _____ . She _____ (have) food at
     13   14
night markets lots of times.

Marta: That's cool!

4 Look at the chart. Then write questions and short answers with the words in parentheses. Use the present perfect.

What have you done?

	play table tennis	do karate	break a bone	act in a play	be on TV	chat online
Emily	✓			✓		✓
Ken		✓	✓			✓
Sandra		✓		✓		✓
Marcos		✓		✓	✓	✓
Julia	✓			✓		

1. (Emily / break a bone)

   Question: *Has Emily ever broken a bone* ? Answer: *No, she hasn't* .

2. (Emily and Ken / be on TV)

   Q: _____ ? A: _____ .

3. (Ken / play table tennis)

   Q: _____ ? A: _____ .

4. (Sandra / do karate)

   Q: _____ ? A: _____ .

5. (Marcos / chat online)

   Q: _____ ? A: _____ .

6. (Marcos and Julia / act in a play)

   Q: _____ ? A: _____ .

5 Look at the chart in Exercise 4. Write sentences about what you have and haven't done. Use *never* for negative sentences.

Example: *I've played table tennis lots of times.*

   I've never done karate.

1. _____

2. _____

3. _____

4. _____

5. _____

6. _____

B *What I mean is, . . .*

1 Cross out the expression that doesn't belong in each list.

1. Are you saying . . .   Do you mean . . .   What I mean is, . . .

2. Do you mean . . .   What I'm saying is, . . .   I mean . . .

3. What I mean is, . . .   Does that mean . . .   What I'm saying is, . . .

4. What I'm saying is, . . .   Does that mean . . .   Do you mean . . .

5. Does that mean . . .   I mean . . .   Are you saying . . .

6. What I'm saying is, . . .   Are you saying . . .   What I mean is, . . .

2 Circle the correct words to complete the conversation.

Jenny: I'm really sleepy.

Amy: Really? Why?

Jenny: I didn't sleep last night.

Amy: (**Do you mean**)/ **I mean** you didn't get any sleep?
       1

an alarm clock

Jenny: Well, no. **What I mean is,** / **Does that mean** I didn't get *much* sleep.
                                  2

Amy: That's too bad. It was better for me. I couldn't stay awake!

Jenny: **What I'm saying is,** / **Are you saying** that you slept a lot?
                         3

Amy: Well, yes. **I mean** / **Do you mean** I slept all night . . . for about eight hours.
                        4

Jenny: Oh. What time do you usually go to bed?

Amy: I go to bed about 10:00 p.m., and I never use an alarm clock in the morning.

Jenny: **What I mean is,** / **Does that mean** you get up late in the morning?
                        5

Amy: No. . . . **What I'm saying is,** / **Are you saying** I wake up early. I always wake up
                              6
      at 6:00 a.m. I don't need an alarm.

Jenny: That's nice. I never wake up early without an alarm.

Life experiences

1 Look at the pictures of Roger and Mary's trip. Then complete the email with the correct expressions from the box.

climbed a mountain	tried an extreme sport	went to a spa
tried an exotic food	✓ went camping	went whale-watching

1.

2.

3.

4.

5.

6.

Hi Lorena and Bill,

We're having a lot of fun in Canada with our friends. Victoria is a beautiful city. Last weekend we

went camping near the ocean. It was great. We
₁

_____ on Saturday, and we _____
₂ ₃

on Sunday. Roger and I even _____ : zip-lining. You go through the
₄

air from tree to tree! It was exciting!

This week, we're staying in a nice hotel. We had dinner at a very nice restaurant in the hotel last

night. I _____ . I ate broiled rainbow trout with fiddleheads and rice.
₅

Rainbow trout is a delicious fish. Fiddleheads are an exotic vegetable. I even

_____ at the hotel with Barbara. Can you believe it? It was very
₆

relaxing. Roger and Tim didn't go.

I have to say good-bye now. We're going to an amusement park in Vancouver, a big city near

Victoria. I can't wait to ride the roller coasters!

Write soon,

Mary

2 Complete the sentences with the correct forms of the words in parentheses. Use the present perfect or the simple past.

1. I _'ve been_ (be) to Mexico lots of times.

2. My sister _____ (eat) at a Turkish restaurant yesterday.

3. Paulina _____ (never / go) to a spa, but I _____ (go) to one last month.

4. _____ you ever _____ (try) an extreme sport?

5. I _____ (try) skiing last year, but I _____ (not / like) it.

6. _____ Jorge and Vanessa _____ (ride) a roller coaster at the park yesterday?

7. What countries _____ you _____ (be) to in the past?

8. My cousins _____ (go) camping last week, but I _____ (never / go) camping before.

3 Write questions to complete the conversations. Use the present perfect and the simple past.

A. Hyun-ju: Hey, Matt. _Have you ever gone camping_____ ?
1

    Matt: No, I haven't. But my sister went camping last weekend.

Hyun-ju: Really? _____ ?
2

    Matt: Yes, she did. She had a lot of fun.

Hyun-ju: _____ ?
3

    Matt: No. She didn't climb a mountain, but she went kayaking.

Hyun-ju: Wow! _____ ?
4

    Matt: No, I have never gone kayaking. But I'd like to go sometime.

Hyun-ju: Me too!

B.   **Josh:** How was your vacation, Nicky?

  Nicky: It was great! _____ ?
1

    Josh: No, I didn't get your postcard. _____ ?
2

  Nicky: I sent it on Monday. It's from Mexico City.

    Josh: Cool!

  Nicky: _____ ?
3

    Josh: Yes, I have. I went to Mexico City last year.

  Nicky: _____ ?
4

    Josh: Yes, I saw the pyramids. They were amazing!

  Nicky: Great! You're going to like my postcard!

4 Look at the chart. Write sentences about what Victor has done using the information in the chart. Use the present perfect or the simple past.

	never	last year	a few years ago	lots of times
1. bowl		✓		
2. play golf			✓	
3. do yoga	✓			
4. join a gym			✓	
5. lift weights				✓
6. climb a mountain	✓			
7. play soccer				✓
8. try karate		✓		

1. _Victor bowled last year._

2. _He_

3. _____

4. _____

5. _____

6. _____

7. _____

8. _____

5 Answer the questions with your own information. Write complete sentences. If your answer is no, add more information.

Example: _Yes, I have. I found it on the beach._ or
No, I haven't. I don't take my phone on vacation.

1. Have you ever lost your phone on vacation? If yes, did you find it?

_____

2. Did you go on vacation last year? If yes, where did you go?

_____

3. Have you ever tried an extreme sport? If yes, did you like it?

_____

4. Have you ever won an award? If yes, why did you win it?

_____

5. Have you ever met a famous person? If yes, who did you meet?

_____

6. Have you ever gotten seasick? If yes, where were you?

_____

D What a life!

1 Read the article. Write the correct question from the box before each answer.

| Is it dangerous? | Are *caving* and *spelunking* different? | What is spelunking? |

The Life of a Spelunker

We interviewed Karen Osgood, a woman who has been spelunking for over 15 years. Read what she says about this interesting activity.

Q: _____
 ₁

A: *Spelunking* is another word for *caving*. It's an interesting activity. People go in caves and walk around in them. For example, I walk around and look at the rocks in caves, and I take pictures. I often have to walk through water, and I sometimes see waterfalls in caves. There is a lot of climbing, too.

Q: _____
 ₂

A: No, not really. Well, what I mean is that some people say *cavers* are serious about the activity and *spelunkers* aren't. They say *spelunkers* go in caves for sport or fun and *cavers* go in caves to explore and learn new things. But many people use the two words in the same way. Of course, scientists who study caves for their job are called speleologists. They know a lot about biology, physics, and chemistry. I'm not a speleologist, but I know a lot about caves. I'm serious about it, too, so I guess I'm a caver. But it's OK if you call me a spelunker!

Q: _____
 ₃

A: Yes, it is. People need to be very careful. Caves are often wet because of water, and you can fall down. You should also wear safe hats and good boots. You sometimes need to wear warm clothing because caves are usually cold. It's very important to take lights, too. You can't see anything without them. I have a light on my hat, so I don't have to hold one in my hand. Oh, and never go in a cave alone. I always explore caves with two or three other people.

2 Read the article again. Then write T (true) or F (false).

1. Karen has been spelunking for many years. __*T*__

2. People don't climb in caves. _____

3. There's sometimes water in caves. _____

4. Spelunkers study caves as part of their job. _____

5. There isn't a lot of light in caves. _____

6. You should always go caving with other people. _____

Our world

A *Older, taller, and more famous*

1 Label the things in the picture with the correct words.

1. c_anal_____

2. b_____

3. tu_____

4. p_____

5. su_____
   sy_____

6. to_____

7. sk_____

8. st_____

2 **Put the words in the correct order to make sentences.**

1. is / the Akashi-Kaikyo Bridge in Japan / older / The Tower Bridge in England / than / .

   The Tower Bridge in England is older than the Akashi-Kaikyo Bridge in Japan.

2. the Erie Canal in the United States / than / is / The Murray Canal in Canada / shorter / .

   _____

3. more / The Sydney Harbor Bridge in Australia / is / than / modern / the Tower Bridge
   in England / .

   _____

4. as / long / the Channel Tunnel between England and France / The Lincoln Tunnel
   between New Jersey and New York City / is / not / as / .

   _____

5. tall / the Sears Tower in the United States / is / The Jin Mao Tower in China / not /
   as / as / .

   _____

6. the London Underground / people on it / has / The New York City subway system /
   more / than / .

   _____

7. as / as / large / the Zócalo square in Mexico City / is / The Plaza Mayor in Madrid /
   not / .

   _____

3 **Circle the correct words to complete the paragraphs.**

There are many skyscrapers in Hong Kong. Two very tall skyscrapers
are the Bank of China Tower and Central Plaza. Central Plaza is
more tall than / (**taller than**) the Bank of China Tower. It also has
                    1
more floors than / **more floors** the Bank of China Tower. The Bank
                    2
of China Tower is **older than** / **older** Central Plaza. But it looks
                    3
more modern / **more modern than** Central Plaza.
                4
I. M. Pei created the Bank of China Tower, and Dennis Lau and Ng
Chun Man created Central Plaza. Some people say that I. M. Pei has
created **more famous buildings than** / **more than famous buildings**
                                    5
Dennis Lau and Ng Chun Man. He has made buildings around the
world. For example, he made the John F. Kennedy Library in Boston
and the pyramid at the Louvre Museum in Paris.

Bank of China Tower   Central Plaza

4 Read about the bridges. Then write comparisons with the words in parentheses. Use *-er* endings or *more . . . than.*

The Brooklyn Bridge, New York City

The Golden Gate Bridge, San Francisco

1. The Brooklyn Bridge is 1,825 meters long. The Golden Gate Bridge is 2,737 meters long. (is / long)

   The Golden Gate Bridge is longer than the Brooklyn Bridge.

2. The Brooklyn Bridge is 26 meters wide. The Golden Gate Bridge is 27 meters wide. (is / wide)

   _____

3. The Brooklyn Bridge opened in 1883. The Golden Gate Bridge opened in 1937. (is / old)

   _____

4. The cost to build the Brooklyn Bridge was $15.5 million. The Golden Gate Bridge was $35 million. (was / expensive)

   _____

5. It took 13 years to build the Brooklyn Bridge. It took four years to build the Golden Gate Bridge. (took / time to build)

   _____

6. Each day, 145,000 people go on the Brooklyn Bridge. Each day, 118,000 people go on the Golden Gate Bridge. (has / people on it each day)

   _____

5 Change sentences 1–4 from Exercise 3. Use *not as . . . as.*

1. *The Brooklyn Bridge is not as long as the Golden Gate Bridge.*

2. _____

3. _____

4. _____

B I don't believe it!

1 Complete the conversation. Use expressions for expressing disbelief and for saying you don't know. The first letter of each word is given.

Tyler: Hey, Susana, look at this.

Susana: What is it?

Tyler: It's information about the plazas in Mexico. There are more plazas in Mexico than anywhere else in the world!

Susana: *I don't believe it!*
1

Tyler: And we're in a very famous plaza – the Zócalo. Do you know another name for it?

Susana: I h_____ n_____ i_____ .
2

Tyler: It's also called Constitution Plaza.

Susana: That's interesting. But I like the name Zócalo better. . . . How old is it?

Tyler: I r_____ d_____ k_____ . But the plaza is older than
3
some of the buildings around it.

Susana: S_____ ?
4

Tyler: Yeah. There used to be different buildings around the plaza, but over the years people built new buildings in place of some of the old ones.

Susana: N_____ w_____ ! I wonder why the old ones are gone. . . .
5
Hey, do you know how big the square is?

Tyler: It says here it's 240 meters long and 240 meters wide.

Susana: That's pretty big! Hey, I'm hungry. Is there a restaurant near the plaza?

Tyler: I d_____ h_____ a c_____ ! Maybe there are some
6
ideas in this book.

2 Complete the conversations with one of the expressions from Exercise 1. More than one answer is possible.

1. **A:** Do you know how long the Channel Tunnel is?

   B: _____

2. **A:** Wow! Did you know the Weihe Grand Bridge is the longest bridge in the world?

   B: _____

C · *World geography*

1 Complete the puzzle with words for geographical features. What's the mystery word?

1.

2.

3.

4.

5.

6.

```
                              ¹R  I  V  E  R
        2 ☐ ☐ ☐ ☐ ☐ ☐
                        3 ☐       ☐ ☐
                        4 ☐       ☐
        5 ☐ ☐ ☐
                              6 ☐ ☐ ☐ ☐ ☐
```

2 Complete the sentences with words for geographical features.

1. The Nile _____*River*_____ is 6,650 kilometers long.

2. A _____ is extremely dry and hot.

3. We swam in a small _____ on vacation.

4. The Indian _____ has less water than the Atlantic or Pacific.

5. Maui is a beautiful _____ surrounded by the Pacific Ocean.

6. I went to the Amazon _____ _____ last winter.
   The trees and other plants were beautiful, and I saw a lot of animals, but it
   really rained a lot!

7. When we went camping last summer, we put up our tent in a _____
   next to a river. Every morning, we looked up at the mountains all around us. It was great!

8. The most famous _____ in the United States is Niagara Falls.

3 Complete the text with the correct superlative forms of the adjectives in parentheses.

YOSEMITE NATIONAL PARK

Yosemite National Park is one of __the most beautiful__ (beautiful)
¹
parks in the United States, and it's one of _____
²
(large) parks in California. There are many interesting geographical
features in Yosemite. Yosemite Valley is _____
³
(popular) place to visit in the park. It's easy to walk around in the
valley. Tuolumne River is _____ (long) river in the
⁴
park, and there are many river trips you can take. There are also many
waterfalls to see in the park. Yosemite Falls is _____ (high) waterfall.
⁵
Chilnualna Falls is one of _____ (difficult) to see because it's behind rocks.
⁶

January, February, and March are _____ (wet) months in Yosemite. Spring
⁷
is _____ (good) season to see waterfalls. Summer is
⁸
_____ (hot) season, and it's also the _____ (busy)
⁹   ¹⁰
season. There aren't many visitors in the park in the winter because it's very cold.

4 Look at the chart. Write sentences with superlative nouns.

In the Caribbean			
	Aruba	**Cuba**	**the Dominican Republic**
1. land	180 km²	110,860 km²	48,670 km²
2. people	104,589	11,477,459	9,794,487
3. rain (each year)	21.3 inches	52 inches	54.5 inches
4. official languages	2	1	1
5. TV stations	1	58	25

1. _Cuba has the most land._ _____

2. _____

3. _____

4. _____

5. _____

5 Complete the sentences with the superlative forms of the underlined words.

1. **A:** We're going to New Guinea this year. It's an extremely large island.

   B: Yes, it is. But Greenland is *the largest*_____ island in the world.

Greenland

2. **A:** This street has a lot of cars. Is there always this much traffic?

   B: Yes, First Avenue gets *the most traffic*_____ in the city.

3. **A:** My uncle does research in the Antarctic Desert, and he says it's really cold.

   B: I know. The Antarctic Desert is _____ desert in the world.

4. **A:** What a great day! Let's sit in the sunshine.

   B: OK. This is _____ we've had all summer!

5. **A:** Wow, this is beautiful! We're up so high. What a great view!

   B: Did you know Lake Titicaca is one of _____ lakes in the world?

6. **A:** I'm going to Japan. Where is a good place to see temples?

   B: I think Kyoto is one of _____ places to see temples in Japan.

7. **A:** I'm tired of being wet on this vacation! It has rained every day on this trip.

   B: Well, May is usually _____ month in this city.

8. **A:** How many people live in New York?

   B: Over 8 million. It's the city in the United States with _____ .

6 Answer the questions with your own information. Write complete sentences and use superlatives.

Example: __*The longest bridge I've ever been on is the Golden Gate Bridge.*__

1. What's the longest bridge you've ever been on? _____

2. Where's the highest place you've ever been? _____

3. What's the most beautiful place you've ever seen? _____

4. Where's the hottest place you've ever been? _____

5. What's the tallest building in your town? _____

6. What's the longest river in your country? _____

7. Which city in your country has the most people? _____

8. Which month gets the most rain in your town? _____

D Natural wonders

1 Read the article. Then write the name of the correct natural wonder under each picture.

1. _____ 2. _____ 3. _____

Canada's Seven Wonders

In 2007, the CBC TV and radio stations had a contest to choose the Seven Wonders of Canada. People sent their ideas to a website and voted for their favorites.

People's Choices	Votes
Sleeping Giant: This is a long peninsula in Lake Superior, which means it has water on three sides. From across the lake, it looks like a big, sleeping person!	177,305
Niagara Falls: These amazing waterfalls are on the border of Canada and the United States. There are three waterfalls, but the largest and most beautiful is called Horseshoe Falls, and most of it is in Canada.	81,818
Bay of Fundy: This is a large body of water where the Atlantic Ocean meets part of Canada. It has the highest tides in the world. The water from the ocean comes in 17 meters higher than when it goes out!	67,670
Nahanni National Park Reserve: This beautiful national park in northern Canada has rivers, waterfalls, mountains, forests, birds, fish, and other animals.	64,920
Northern Lights: These are colorful moving lights in the sky. The best time to see them is on very dark, cool nights in March, April, September, and October.	61,417
The Rockies: The Canadian Rockies are beautiful, high mountains that have sharp peaks and wide valleys. They are cool and wet, but the tops have no trees because it is too cold and rocky for them to grow.	55,630
Cabot Trail: This 950-kilometer hiking trail through part of the Rockies has some of the most beautiful views in Canada. It is named after John Cabot, an Italian man who explored the land in 1497.	44,073

2 Read the article again. Then answer the questions.

1. When was the contest for the Seven Wonders of Canada? _____ *2007* _____

2. Which place had the most votes? _____

3. Which ocean's water goes into the Bay of Fundy? _____

4. What are the best months to see the northern lights? _____

5. How long is the Cabot Trail? _____

Organizing your time

A *A busy week*

1 Complete the phone conversations with words from the box.

✓birthday	business	doctor's	soccer
blind	conference	job	violin

A. **Jake:** Hey, Ramon. Can you come to my

_____*birthday*_____ party on Saturday?

1

Ramon: I'm not sure. I have a _____

2

appointment at the hospital at 2:00 p.m. What

time is the party?

Jake: It starts at 4:00 p.m. And there's someone

I want you to meet. Her name is Olivia.

Ramon: Well, I can come to the party. But I don't know about Olivia. I've never

been on a _____ date.

3

Jake: It's not really a date. You're both just going to be at the party. It'll be fun!

B. **Yae-jih:** Hi, Don. How are you?

Don: OK. I'm a little nervous about my _____ interview at TGL Bank.

1

Yae-jih: Oh, right. When is it?

Don: Today at 2:00. Mr. Lawrence and Mrs. Nelson have a lot of _____

2

meetings, so we are going to have a _____ call. I won't have an

3

interview face-to-face.

Yae-jih: Wow. That's different. Good luck!

C. **Laura:** Hello, Sibel. Do you want to have lunch tomorrow?

Sibel: I'm sorry. I can't. I have a _____ lesson tomorrow.

1

How about on Saturday?

Laura: I have _____ practice in the afternoon.

2

Let's have dinner on Saturday night.

Sibel: OK, great. And we can go to a movie after dinner, too.

2 Circle the correct words to complete the email.

Hi Jim,

How are you? Thanks for your email. It will be great to see you next week. What **(are you doing)** / **do you do** on Thursday? I have tickets to a hip-hop concert, if you'd like to go with me. **It's starting** / **It starts** at 8:00 p.m. **I'm having** / **I have** soccer practice at 4:00, but **it's ending** / **it ends** at 5:30. If you can go to the concert, we could meet for dinner at 6:30 at Oh Boy Pizza. What do you think?

Are you busy on July 28th? **I'm moving** / **I move** that day. Could you help me move? Katie and Mike **are helping** / **help** me, too. They **are going** / **go** to a yoga class every Saturday from 8:00 to 10:00 a.m., so we'll start at 11:00. **I'm buying** / **I buy** lunch for everyone.

I hope you can go to the concert. Write soon or call me!

Raul

3 Check (✓) the correct sentences. Rewrite the incorrect sentences with the correct forms of the verbs. Use the simple present or the present continuous.

1. ☐ Lorena is having a violin lesson every Thursday.

   Lorena has a violin lesson every Thursday.

2. ☐ Do you have any doctor's appointments next week?

   _____

3. ☐ Marvin picks up his sister in Miami at 3:30 p.m. on Saturday.

   _____

4. ☐ Brenda and Tom are staying at my house this weekend.

   _____

5. ☐ Naoki plans a conference call in meeting room B for Tuesday next week.

   _____

6. ☐ The movie starts at 9:00 and is ending at 11:30.

   _____

4 Read the sentences. Check (✓) if the event is happening right now or in the future.

	Now	Future
1. I can't have lunch now. I'm studying for my biology test.	✓	☐
2. I have a doctor's appointment on Friday.	☐	☐
3. Jen is working late next week.	☐	☐
4. I'm eating a great sandwich. Do you want to try it?	☐	☐
5. I'm sorry. Tae Jung isn't here. He has soccer practice.	☐	☐
6. Melanie can't go on a blind date on Saturday. She has a guitar lesson.	☐	☐
7. We're leaving for vacation in three days!	☐	☐
8. Larry isn't answering his cell phone. He is on a conference call.	☐	☐

5 Complete the calendar with your own plans for next week. Write sentences with the present continuous or the simple present.

Example: **Sunday:** _I have gymnastics practice._ or _I'm visiting my aunt and uncle._

WEEKLY CALENDAR

Sunday	
Monday	
Tuesday	
Wednesday	
Thursday	
Friday	
Saturday	

B *Can I take a message?*

1 Put the words in the correct order to make sentences for leaving and offering to take phone messages.

1. leave / want / a / message / to / you / Do / ?   *Do you want to leave a message?*

2. Amber called / him / Please / tell / that / .   _____

3. is at 12:15 / the conference call / her / Can / you / tell / that / ?   _____

4. know / in the morning / that / you / her / Could / let / we're leaving / ?   _____

5. like / to / you / Would / leave / message / a / ?   _____

6. take / a / message / I / Can / ?   _____

2 Complete the conversations with sentences from Exercise 1. Each sentence in Exercise 1 is used once. Sometimes, the first word is given.

A. **Brandon:** Hello?

　Amber: Hi. Can I speak to Jim?

　Brandon: I'm sorry. He's not here. Do
　　　　you want to leave a message ?
　　　　　　　　　　1

　Amber: Sure. _____
　　　　　　　　　2

　　　　_____ .

> **While You Were Out**
>
> For: *Jim*　　　　Date: *October 2*
>
> Message: *Amber called.*
> *909-555-1234*
>
> _____
>
> _____

B. **Victoria:** Hello?

　Marcos: Hello. Can I speak to Tonya, please?

　Victoria: Um, she's busy right now. Can _____ ?
　　　　　　　　　　　　　　　　　　　　　1

　Marcos: Yes. We have a business meeting at work tomorrow.

　　　　_____ ?
　　　　　　　　　　2

　Victoria: 12:15. OK. No problem.

C. **Emma:** Hello?

　Asami: Hi. Is Kendra there?

　Emma: No, she isn't. Would _____ ?
　　　　　　　　　　　　　　　　　1

　Asami: Oh, sure. I'm picking her up tomorrow for a camping trip.

　　　　_____ ?
　　　　　　　　　　2

　Emma: OK. What time?

　Asami: About 10:00 a.m.

C Can you do me a favor?

1 Circle the correct phrase to complete each conversation.

1. **A:** Algebra is difficult.

   B: Do you want some help?

   A: Yes. Can you **help me with my résumé** / **check my homework**?

2. **A:** That restaurant is too expensive.

   B: I know, but the food is really good. Let's go.

   A: Well, OK. Could you **lend me some money** / **water my plants**?

3. **A:** Hi, Ed. It's Sherry.

   B: Hi, Sherry. You're calling me early. Is there a problem?

   A: Yes. My car isn't working. Can you **check my homework** / **give me a ride to work**?

4. **A:** Look at those flowers! Your garden is so beautiful!

   B: Thanks. Would you mind **watering the plants** / **getting the mail** with me?

5. **A:** Julia is so nice. She always wants to help.

   B: I know. She's **feeding my cat** / **giving me a ride** while I'm on vacation.

6. **A:** Do you want to go to a movie tonight?

   B: I'm sorry, I can't. I'm **getting my mail** / **picking up my parents at the airport**.

7. **A:** I need to find a job.

   B: My office needs some new workers.

   A: Really? That's great. Could you **help me with my résumé** / **pick me up**?

8. **A:** Does anyone stay at your house when you travel for work?

   B: No. My neighbor usually **gets my mail** / **checks my homework**.
   And he also feeds my fish.

2 Complete the conversation with words from the box.

✓can you do	I'll clean	I won't forget	would you mind cleaning
could you take	I'll cook	Would you make	

Tina: Matt, _can you do_ _____ me a favor?
                                 1

Matt: Sure, Tina. What is it?

Tina: I'm going to be home late tonight, around 7:00.
         _____ dinner?
                      2

Matt: No problem. _____ tacos
                          3
and rice and beans.

Tina: Oh, that sounds great! And _____
                                        4
_____ out the garbage? It has to go out tonight.

Matt: Definitely. _____ . I promise!
                           5

Tina: Thanks. Oh, and _____ the apartment? Our new
                               6
neighbors, Jay and Camille, are coming over for dinner. Remember?

Matt: Um, OK. I guess _____ it before I make dinner.
                              7

Tina: Thanks. You're the best!

3 Rewrite the questions. Use *would you mind*. Then complete the responses with *will*.

1. Can you check my homework?

   A: _Would you mind checking my homework?_

   B: No problem. _I'll check_ _____ it after dinner.

2. Could you pick me up at 10:30 a.m.?

   A: _____

   B: Not at all. _____ at any time you want me to.

3. Would you give me a ride to my doctor's appointment?

   A: _____

   B: No problem. _____ you a ride in my new car!

4. Would you tell Josh that the meeting is tomorrow?

   A: _____

   B: No, I don't mind. _____ him when I see him at lunch.

5. Could you water the plant in my office while I'm out next week?

   A: _____

   B: No problem. _____ it. How often should I do it?

4 Look at Eric's notes. Then complete his conversation with each person.

give me a ride to the airport	Priscilla
feed my fish	Chuck
feed my cat	Chuck
get my mail	Amira
pick me up from the airport	Greg

1.   **Eric:** Can you give me a ride to the airport on Monday afternoon?

   Priscilla: No problem. *I'll give you a ride to the airport.* What time?

2.   **Eric:** Can _____ while I'm on a trip next week?

   Chuck: Sure. _____ them.

   Eric: And would you mind _____ , too?

   Chuck: No, I don't mind. _____ it, too.

3.   **Eric:** Would _____ when I'm on my trip?

   Amira: All right. _____ it on Wednesday and Friday.

4.   **Eric:** Could _____ at 4:30 on Sunday?

   Greg: Yeah, sure. _____ and _____ be late!

5 People are asking you favors. Write their questions and your own answers.

1.   **Ed:** *Can you take my picture* ?

   You: _____ .

2.   **Mai:** _____ ?

   You: _____ .

3.   **Chris:** _____ ?

   You: _____ .

4.   **Mara:** _____ ?

   You: _____ .

D Time management

1 Read the article. What are four ways that people waste time?

1. _the Internet_   2. _____   3. _____   4. _____

A Waste of Time!

Many people don't manage their time well. They often find other things to do when they should be working. Some people don't even know they are wasting time. These are some of the top time-wasters. Do any of them sound like you?

1. The Internet is a very useful tool, but it's also the biggest way people waste time. Many people play games or chat online instead of working or doing research for school. Have you ever looked at a funny video online instead of working?

2. TV can be interesting and educational, but many people waste time by watching TV. Have you ever taken a short break from work to watch "just a little TV" and then hours later thought, "Oh, that's right. . . . I was doing laundry."?

3. People can actually waste a lot of time when they talk. At work, some people talk too much about personal things instead of doing their jobs. Other people have the same problem at home. They talk to friends and family on the phone instead of doing chores.

4. Believe it or not, thinking can be a waste of time. Some people think about work, but they don't do it. They even make to-do lists, but then they just think about all the things they have to do, and they never get them done!

2 Read the article again and the sentences below. Did each person waste time?
Check (✓) Yes or No.

	Yes	No
1. Vicky researched information on the Internet for a work report.	☐	✓
2. Dan played a game online for two hours at work.	☐	☐
3. Ines watched TV for ten minutes and then finished her homework.	☐	☐
4. Haluk talked to his boss about a business meeting.	☐	☐
5. Sam talked to his boss about his son's soccer game.	☐	☐
6. Jen made a to-do list, and then she thought about how she'd never finish all of it.	☐	☐